STRUCTURED
Writing II

Using Inspiration Software to Teach Essay Development

Kathleen McMurdo

International Society for Technology in Education
EUGENE, OREGON

Structured Writing II
Using Inspiration Software to Teach Essay Development

Kathleen McMurdo

Director of Publishing
Jean Marie Hall

Acquisitions Editors
Mathew Manweller
Scott Harter

Production Editor
Tracy Cozzens

Copy Editor
Lynne Ertle

Cover Design
Signe Landin

Inside Design
Kim McGovern

Layout and Production
Tracy Cozzens
Signe Landin
Kim McGovern

International Society for Technology in Education (ISTE)
480 Charnelton Street
Eugene, OR 97401-2626
Order Desk: 1.800.336.5191
Order Fax: 1.541.302.3778
Customer Service: orders@iste.org
Books and Courseware: books@iste.org
Permissions: permissions@iste.org
World Wide Web: www.iste.org

First Edition
ISBN 1-56484-179-0

About ISTE

The International Society for Technology in Education (ISTE) is a nonprofit professional organization with a worldwide membership of leaders in educational technology. We are dedicated to promoting appropriate uses of information technology to support and improve learning, teaching, and administration in PK–12 education and teacher education. As part of that mission, ISTE provides high-quality and timely information, services, and materials, such as this book.

The ISTE Publishing Department works with experienced educators to develop and produce classroom-tested books and courseware. We look for content that emphasizes the use of technology where it can make a difference— making the teacher's job easier; saving time; motivating students; helping students who have unique learning styles, abilities, or backgrounds; and creating learning environments that would be impossible without technology. We believe technology can improve the effectiveness of teaching while making learning exciting and fun.

Every manuscript and product we select for publication is peer reviewed and professionally edited. While we take pride in our publications, we also recognize the difficulties of maintaining quality while keeping on top of the latest technologies and research. Please let us know which products you would find helpful. We value your feedback on this book and other ISTE products. E-mail us at **books@iste.org**.

ISTE is home of the National Educational Technology Standards (NETS) Project, the National Educational Computing Conference (NECC), and the National Center for Preparing Tomorrow's Teachers to Use Technology (NCPT[3]). To learn more about NETS or request a print catalog, visit our Web site at **www.iste.org**, which provides:

- Current educational technology standards for PK–12 students, teachers, and administrators

- A bookstore with online ordering and membership discount options

- *Learning & Leading with Technology* magazine and the *Journal of Research on Technology in Education*

- *ISTE Update,* online membership newsletter

- Teacher resources

- Discussion groups

- Professional development services, including national conference information

- Research projects

- Member services

About the Author

Kathleen McMurdo is a special education instructor at Chartwell School, a special day school for children ages 7 through 14 who are challenged with dyslexia and related learning disabilities. She has worked as a teacher at Chartwell School for the past 13 years, and collaborated there with Charles Haynes, technology coordinator. Together, they developed innovative courses for students and teachers that link direct instruction of the writing process with computer use. From this work, the Structured Writing process has developed.

McMurdo has presented the Structured Writing techniques extensively at education conferences including the International Dyslexia Association; the Learning Disabilities Association; Computer Using Educators (CUE); and Technology, Reading, and Learning Difficulties (TRLD). McMurdo received her bachelor of arts degree at San Jose State University and her master of arts degree in special education, specializing in the learning handicapped field, from Chapman University. She has a California Resource Specialist Certification, is Slingerland trained, and teaches the Orton-Gillingham sequence.

Inspired by the struggles of her son, who has dyslexia and is an alumnus of Chartwell, McMurdo completed her degrees as a re-entry student with the intention of working specifically with students who have learning disabilities. She resides in Carmel, California.

About Write:OutLoud

The author recommends, but does not require, the use of Write:OutLoud word processing software in the Structured Writing II program. The following describes Write:OutLoud software.

Write:OutLoud was originally designed to help students with physical or learning disabilities. However, teachers report that Write:OutLoud motivates all students to write more. The program is so versatile and powerful, it can be used by students through Grade 12. To help increase schools' effectiveness with version control, installation, and administration, a network version is available.

Write:OutLoud is a talking word processor. As your students write, the program visually highlights and says the letters, words, and sentences on the screen. The program's combined visual and auditory reinforcement gives your students immediate feedback on their writing. By hearing the words and seeing the highlighting, students can self-correct their writing and work independently.

To further develop independent writing skills, Write:OutLoud comes with the Franklin Dictionary with Homonym Checker and the Franklin Spell Checker. Students can consult the on-screen dictionary to check a word's meaning or to find the right word to use. When they have finished writing, the spelling checker identifies and corrects spelling errors, including most phonetic spelling errors. Because of these features, as students use Write:OutLoud to improve their writing, they will also see improvements in their reading, spelling, and vocabulary.

Write:OutLoud is an easy-to-use tool that students can use throughout the writing process, from brainstorming ideas through first drafts to final polishing, formatting, and printing. To keep students focused on writing, Write:OutLoud uses on-screen tool icons instead of menu selections to simplify the use of the word processor.

You may contact Don Johnston at:

Don Johnston
26799 W. Commerce Dr.
Volo, IL 60073
Tel. 1.800.999.4660
Fax 1.847.740.7326
www.donjohnston.com

Contents

Introduction

Writing skills are fundamental for success in elementary school, middle school, high school, and college. Yet many struggling students, perhaps because of a lack of reading experience or other academic difficulties, haven't a clue where to start or how to write a paragraph, much less an essay. Many students also demonstrate organizational problems, handwriting difficulties, or a combination of the two. These further decrease the probability of successful completion of written assignments. A large population of teachers and struggling students has been searching for assistance with writing instruction. My previous book, *Structured Writing* (written in collaboration with Charles Haynes), provides teachers and students with a fully articulated process for developing structurally sound sentences and paragraphs. *Structured Writing* provides explicit expectations and uses step-by-step, direct instruction of the writing process to help students successfully write a variety of paragraphs.

The purpose of this new book, *Structured Writing II—Using Inspiration Software to Teach Essay Development,* is to expand the process and use it to teach students to develop written essays and reports. Once students have mastered writing basic paragraphs and the various types of expanded paragraphs in *Structured Writing,* they are ready for more challenging writing assignments. Prior experience using the Structured Writing process simplifies this transition to writing longer, more complex pieces. *Structured Writing II* connects the students' previously learned knowledge about writing paragraphs and applies it to written essays and reports.

Structured Writing II permits struggling students to produce structurally correct essays and reports that meet teacher expectations and requirements. The basic structure of a five-sentence paragraph is dissected and the components expanded to a five-paragraph essay. The essential elements of an essay are explained using the essential elements of a paragraph. The topic sentence in a paragraph becomes the focus statement in the essay's introductory paragraph. The three supporting sentences in the basic paragraph become the topic sentences for each of the three supporting paragraphs in the essay. Additionally, the paragraph's concluding sentence becomes the basis for the concluding paragraph in the essay.

PARAGRAPH	ESSAY
Topic Sentence	Introductory Paragraph
First Supporting Sentence	First Supporting Paragraph
Second Supporting Sentence	Second Supporting Paragraph
Third Supporting Sentence	Third Supporting Paragraph
Concluding Sentence	Concluding Paragraph

The writing process remains the same throughout all written assignments. The various types of essays replicate the types of paragraphs previously learned in *Structured Writing*. Writing simple essays evolves to developing more complex essays and reports.

New elements of an essay are identified, explained, and connected to previously learned concepts, one at a time. Special paragraph types (such as introductory and concluding paragraphs) are introduced and their functions explained. The purpose of the essay, the intended audience, and a plan of delivery must also be considered when organizing paragraphs in an essay, and these elements are addressed at appropriate points in the process. New strategies to improve vocabulary and innovative techniques for writing sincere, snappy, interesting, thoughtful, or humorous introductory and concluding paragraphs are also discussed.

Structured Writing II uses computer technology to emphasize each of the basic writing steps: planning, writing, editing, formatting, and publishing. Inspiration software is used to plan and organize ideas in the planning step. In Inspiration, each paragraph is broken down into a color-coded outline with structure cues for required elements: topic sentence, supporting sentences, details, and concluding sentence. Similar color-coded computer templates or "webs" show the overall structure of specific essay types and the order of the individual paragraphs within them.

Word processing programs (such as Write:OutLoud) are then used to write, edit, and revise the sentences, paragraphs, and essays. Word processing templates used in the writing step include teacher-created organizers that match the structure and color code of the Inspiration outlines. Keyboarding allows students to produce legible text and eliminate handwriting difficulties. Text-to-speech features and spelling checkers are employed in a sequential, methodical way to improve content and help editing accuracy. Students also use the thesaurus to improve the complexity and sophistication of their vocabulary in the editing step. Computer technology is then also used for the final steps, formatting the document appropriately and printing the polished piece.

Structured Writing II encourages good writing practices and emphasizes process before product. Moving through the sequence, you will notice that expectations for sentence variation and complexity increase incrementally. The Structured Writing process has changed the way I teach writing and has proven to be a valuable tool for my students. Their successes have encouraged me to share this process and further develop it. I hope it will help others to teach and produce written assignments that more accurately reflect student knowledge and understanding.

Chapter 1

The Structured Writing Process

Structured Writing is a process that teaches students how to write complete paragraphs using the computer. By combining effective writing instruction with the editing and text-to-speech features of current word processing programs, the Structured Writing process enhances student writing. The computer is a useful tool to teach writing for several reasons. First, the computer allows students to produce neatly printed, accurately spelled, readable text—a professional-looking product that raises self-esteem. Second, the ease with which students can make multiple edits eliminates the tedious and frustrating task of rewriting and revising by hand. Students are free to express themselves and use words they are not sure how to spell, knowing they will edit their writing at the next step. This freedom from tedious handwritten revisions also encourages more elaboration.

Compared with writing a sentence, writing a paragraph can be a daunting task for many students. Writing a paragraph is made more manageable when written sentence by sentence. The Structured Writing process focuses on writing a paragraph one sentence at a time so that students can focus on content and not get discouraged or sidetracked during the writing process. Planning, writing, editing, formatting, and publishing are emphasized as separate steps in the writing process. The teacher can observe the students during the various steps in the writing process, assess individual difficulties, and intervene with instruction immediately, enabling them to guide students efficiently through the difficult process of paragraph writing.

The Structured Writing process also provides students with the organizational help that makes writing effective paragraphs achievable. The color-coded outlines and organizers alert the students to the essential elements of paragraphs and communicate the teacher's expectations. Whether a student has a plethora of ideas to write about or is stifled by writer's block, the Structured Writing process has a place for every thought and element required. It provokes and cues ideas for students who are having difficulty figuring out what to write.

While my first book, *Structured Writing* (written in collaboration with Charles Haynes), explains an effective process of paragraph development using the computer, *Structured Writing II* expands that process to describe and explain methods for combining paragraphs into more complex expository essays and reports. Students, of course, must be able to produce structurally correct sentences before they can write effective paragraphs. In the same way, they need to be familiar with the process of writing complete and structurally sound paragraphs before they can successfully incorporate them into longer essays. I recommend using *Structured Writing* to teach and reinforce the writing process at the paragraph level for all students. The Paragraph Writing Requirements poster at the end of this chapter presents a list of requirements for completing individual paragraphs. Even students who are already proficient writing paragraphs will benefit from a review of the writing process, and *Structured Writing's* emphasis on organization and step-by-step instruction using Inspiration software will help prepare them for the longer essay assignments in *Structured Writing II*. The writing process is largely the same in both books, but the added length and complexity of the essays in *Structured Writing II* provide students with a much greater challenge.

Many students state that they do not know what is expected of them when given a writing assignment. The Structured Writing process gives students explicit instructions and clearly defines the teacher's expectations. Color-coded templates for each type of paragraph or essay have been created to identify the required writing components and format for each assignment, allowing students to see precisely what they need to do to complete it. Experience has shown that explicit, step-by-step instruction increases the chances of success for all writing students. The students in my classes express relief knowing the expectations for a writing assignment, and this makes them more motivated right from the beginning.

Deciding the order in which information is presented in a paragraph is also very difficult for many students. Structured Writing templates define that order and allow students to write paragraphs **one sentence at a time.** Placing words and ideas in the template automatically puts them in the required sequence for each paragraph. Color-coding provides visual reinforcement of the essential elements of individual paragraphs, and each sentence that a student writes is automatically placed in its proper position.

The Five Steps

The Structured Writing process uses five distinct steps to help students generate thoughtful, well-written pieces. Each step contains several elements.

♦ Planning

♦ Writing

♦ Editing

♦ Formatting

♦ Publishing

Planning step. An Inspiration web template is used to organize ideas and generate an outline that will guide the writing.

Writing step. A word processing organizer template is color-coded to match the Inspiration outline, allowing students to expand and organize their ideas into a paragraph, one sentence at a time.

Editing step. Using the editing functions of a word processing program, students correct capitalization, punctuation, misused words, and spelling errors. The writers expand their sentences using modifiers, adjectives, adverbs, and prepositional phrases. Students vary sentence structure and enhance vocabulary by using the thesaurus. The Editing Steps poster at the end of this chapter lists the editing procedures for easy reference. Encourage students to refer to it when they are editing and revising their work.

Formatting step. The structure cues provided in the organizer template are removed from the document, leaving only the students' work. Sentences are placed into paragraph form. Students reread the paragraph as a whole to ensure they have used proper transition words in the supporting sentences, and submit it to a proofreader.

Publishing step. After submission to a proofreader, the document is corrected, the color code removed, and the writing published as a final copy.

The Structured Writing method is a gradual process. For example, in *Structured Writing,* students begin by writing a simple, concrete sentence. One at a time, additional new writing concepts are added to previously learned concepts. The Basic Paragraph is taught before elaborating it into Expanded Paragraphs with specific rhetorical functions: reason, example, process, classification, and compare and contrast. Varying sentence structure and using transitions to separate the supporting sentences are introduced here, as well as using a thesaurus to vary word choice and incorporate a more complex vocabulary. The paragraph webs from the first book are illustrated in the Summary of Webs From *Structured Writing* poster on the foldout page at the end of this chapter.

The following list presents the progression of paragraphs in *Structured Writing*.

STRUCTURED WRITING PARAGRAPH SEQUENCE
◆ Basic Paragraph
◆ Expanded Paragraph
◆ Reason Paragraph
◆ Example Paragraph
◆ Process Paragraph
◆ Classification Paragraph
◆ Compare and Contrast Paragraph

The same gradual progression takes place in *Structured Writing II*. First, students are introduced to two paragraph types that are essential to longer essays and reports, the introductory paragraph and the concluding paragraph. Then, students are guided through the process of turning a single expanded paragraph into a five-paragraph essay, using the individual sentences in the paragraph as topic sentences for the introductory, supporting, and concluding paragraphs of the essay. The Paragraph Web to Essay Web foldout poster at the end of this chapter illustrates this process.

Once students have become familiar and comfortable with this expansion process, they are then asked to produce expository essays based on the reason, example, process, classification, and compare and contrast paragraphs they created using the Structured Writing process. After students have sufficient experience writing expository essays, they turn to the persuasive essay and learn its specific requirements. In the final chapter, students learn how to write three types of book reports.

Useful Rubrics

Each lesson comes with an evaluation rubric for that specific essay type to assist teachers in assessing individual student progress. These rubrics isolate the elements of a complete writing evaluation: structure and organization, mechanics, and content. They are useful for providing specific, positive feedback to writers.

Important Tools

Teachers use specific software for each step to reinforce the sequential nature of the writing process. The following list shows the tools necessary for completing the Structured Writing II process.

STRUCTURED WRITING II TOOLS
Inspiration 6.0 or 7.0
◆ Web template
◆ Outline
Write:OutLoud, Microsoft Word
◆ Organizer template
◆ Editing

Inspiration, a program that allows the use of **webs** and **outlines**, is required for the planning step of the Structured Writing process. Inspiration versions 6.0 and 7.0 are compatible

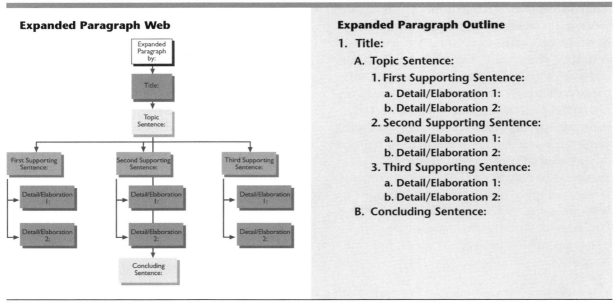

Figure 1. An Inspiration web becomes an outline, the starting point for a written piece.

with the Structured Writing II CD-ROM. If you aren't familiar with Inspiration, the company Web site (www.inspiration.com) provides a 30-day free trial to download a full working version of either Inspiration or Kidspiration. The customized web templates created for the Structured Writing II CD-ROM help students to organize and outline their thoughts and ideas for writing. The templates provide the specific structure required by each type of paragraph, essay, or book report, with essential elements color-coded for easy recognition. This visual representation of the composition as a whole teaches students the basic structure of each paragraph, essay, and report, and reinforces that structure each time the student sits down to write. Figure 1 presents the Inspiration web and outline for the Expanded Paragraph, introduced in *Structured Writing*.

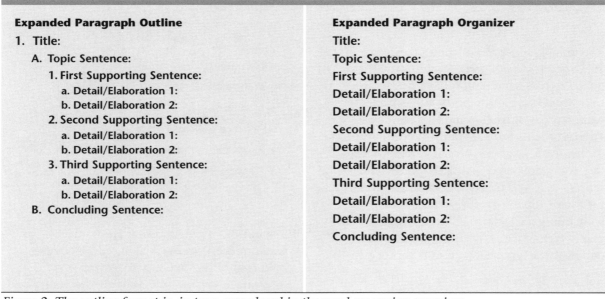

Figure 2. The outline format is, in turn, reproduced in the word processing organizer.

After students outline their ideas using the Inspiration web templates, they use customized word processing **organizer** templates (also on the accompanying CD-ROM) to guide their writing and expand the key words and short phrases from the outline into complete sentences. The color code of the organizer template matches that of the web template to further reinforce the essential elements of the paragraphs and essays. Sentences and paragraphs are composed one at a time in the same sequence as the outline. Figure 2 illustrates the outline and organizer templates for the Expanded Paragraph.

To ensure that students benefit from the built-in organization of the Structured Writing II templates, the word processing program they use must be able to display color text. However, it is not necessary to use or have access to a color printer. Those without access to a color printer can use highlighters to color-code the printed documents. In fact, this is how I developed the Structured Writing process in the first place! It can be good practice for students to identify the essential elements of their own written compositions by color-coding them with highlighters when a color printer is not available.

While a variety of word processing programs are currently used in schools, I recommend that Structured Writing II students use Write:OutLoud, a word processing program developed by Don Johnston, Inc. Write:OutLoud is formatted for both PCs and Macintosh computers, and includes a very useful text-to-speech feature as well as color text. A word processing program with text-to-speech capabilities is extremely important for the editing step because it allows students to simultaneously hear and see their written words. Students are often able to recognize their mistakes more easily when they hear them, which allows them to self-correct their essays better than if they simply look for mistakes in their written work. My struggling students benefit from simultaneous, multisensory feedback, which increases their editing

accuracy as well as their independence while writing. However, any other word processing program that displays color text can be used; on the CD-ROM, I have included organizer templates for use with Microsoft Word or other word processors, as well as Write:OutLoud.

Summary

The Structured Writing process remains the same, regardless of the kind of paragraph or essay that students are asked to write. This consistency of approach—and the familiarity it creates—helps to support struggling students and encourages them to focus their attention on expressing their thoughts and feelings in writing. The ease and manageability of writing a paragraph one sentence at a time is applied to longer compositions in *Structured Writing II,* which shows students how complex essays and reports can be accurately and efficiently written step by step, one paragraph at a time.

Paragraph Writing Requirements

For each assigned paragraph, follow the sequence of steps to get full credit for the assignment.

Planning Step (Outline)

- ☐ Open the Inspiration web template
- ☐ Type key words and short phrases into web
- ☐ Convert into outline format by selecting Outline option
- ☐ Save as "title.outline"
- ☐ Print outline in color or print and highlight by hand
- ☐ Submit to the teacher for review

Writing Step (Organizer)

- ☐ Open the word processing organizer template
- ☐ Expand words/phrases from outline into complete sentences
- ☐ Save as "title.organizer"
- ☐ Print organizer in color or print and highlight by hand
- ☐ Submit to the teacher for review

Editing Step (Edited Organizer)

- ☐ Open the saved organizer, "title.organizer"
- ☐ Read and listen to each sentence
- ☐ Revise sentences for content, and vary sentence structure
- ☐ Check capitalization, punctuation, word usage, and spelling
- ☐ Save as "title.organizer"
- ☐ Read and listen to edited organizer
- ☐ Print organizer in color or print and highlight by hand
- ☐ Submit first to proofreader and then to teacher for review

Formatting Step (Draft)

- ☐ Open the saved organizer, "title.organizer"
- ☐ Highlight and delete structure cues and headings
- ☐ Center title and check for proper capitalization
- ☐ Indent topic sentence and adjust spacing between sentences
- ☐ Save as "title.draft"
- ☐ Read and listen to draft of paragraph
- ☐ Print draft in color or print and highlight by hand
- ☐ Submit to a proofreader for review

Publishing Step (Final)

- ☐ Open saved draft, "title.draft"
- ☐ Make changes suggested by proofreader
- ☐ Remove color code and change text to black
- ☐ SAVE AS "title.final copy"
- ☐ Print
- ☐ Submit a complete package to teacher:
  - ▶ Outline
  - ▶ Organizer
  - ▶ Draft
  - ▶ Final Copy

Editing Steps

1. Open organizer file

2. Read and listen; edit and revise

3. Check capitalization

4. Check punctuation

5. Check word usage

6. Check spelling

7. Read and listen

8. Save

9. Print

10. Submit to proofreader for review

11. Make any necessary changes suggested by the proofreader

12. Submit to teacher for approval

Essay Title:

Concluding Paragraph

- Clincher Sentence Idea:
- Restate Thesis/Focus Sentence Idea:
  - Third Point Summarized:
    - Detail:
  - Second Point Summarized:
    - Detail:
  - First Point Summarized:
    - Detail:

Third Supporting Paragraph

- Concluding Sentence:
- Third Point Topic Sentence Idea and Transition:
  - Third Supporting Idea:
    - Detail:
    - Detail:
    - Detail:
  - Second Supporting Idea:
    - Detail:
    - Detail:
    - Detail:
  - First Supporting Idea:
    - Detail:
    - Detail:
    - Detail:

Second Supporting Paragraph

- Concluding Sentence:
- Third Supporting Idea:

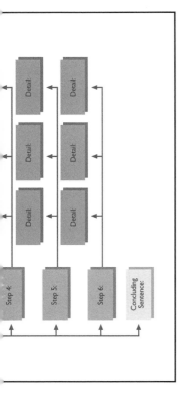

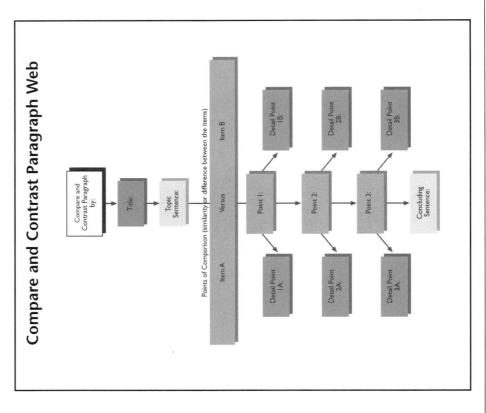

Compare and Contrast Paragraph Web

Classification Paragraph Web

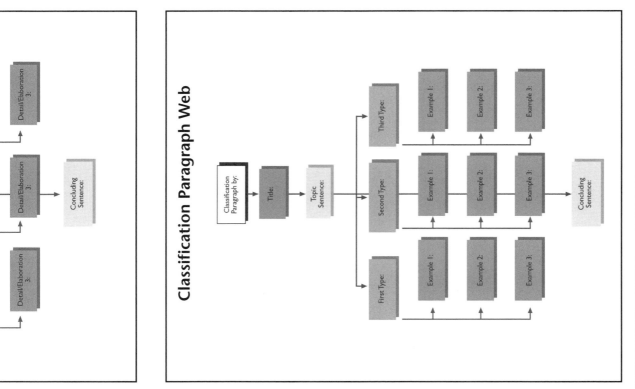

Summary of Webs From Structured Writing

Basic Paragraph Web

Expanded Paragraph Web

Reason Paragraph Web

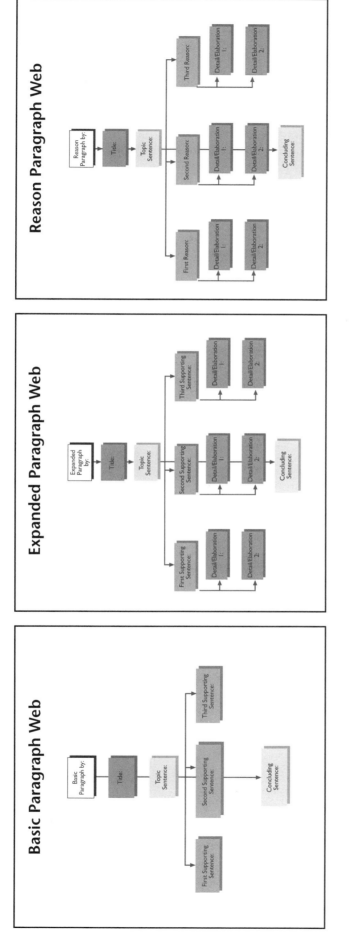

Process Paragraph Web

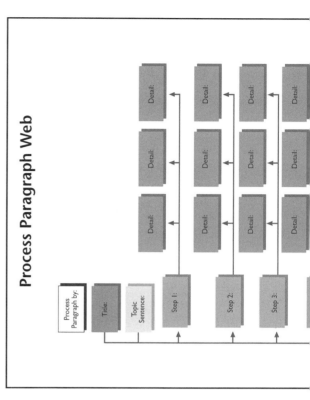

Example Paragraph Web

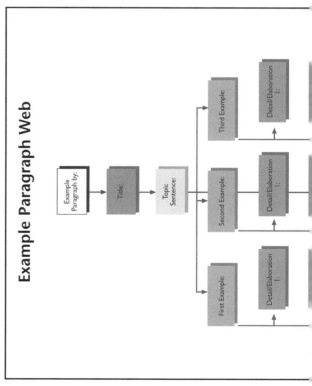

Paragraph Web to Essay Web

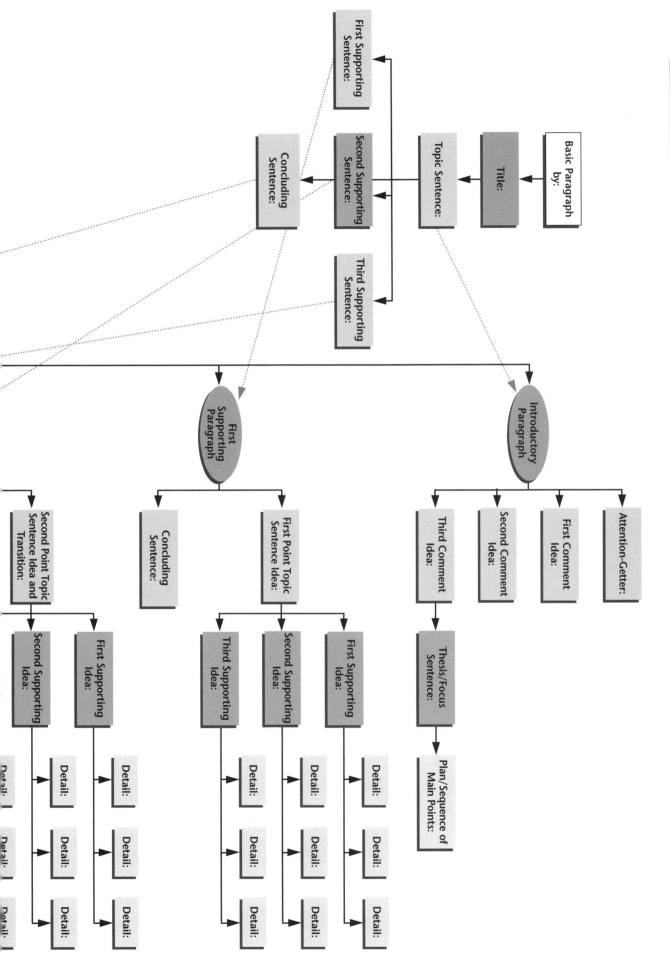

Chapter 2

The Introductory Paragraph

Expository essays and reports require introductory and concluding paragraphs. In the introductory paragraph, writers come up with a main idea that announces the theme of the paper. The purpose of the introductory paragraph is to introduce the subject in an interesting way and state the specific focus of the essay. Introductory paragraphs begin with general comments about the essay topic that entice the reader to read the essay. Writers then use the thesis/focus sentence to specify the essay's topic with more precision. The supporting points are then identified.

Students are encouraged to use many different introductory techniques to get the reader's attention (for ideas, see the Introductory Techniques and Attention-Getters poster at the end of this chapter). These techniques allow students to introduce a specific topic and their own perspective on it in a variety of creative ways.

THESIS/FOCUS SENTENCES

A thesis sentence presents a position to be proven or argued for. A focus sentence describes the specific topic to be discussed. Some expository essays, such as persuasive pieces, require a thesis sentence; others call for a focus sentence that pinpoints the theme. The webs use the term "Thesis/Focus Sentence" to capture both meanings.

Objectives

1. Students will use the Structured Writing technique to draft an introductory paragraph.

2. Students will use the color codes to reinforce the essential elements of the introductory paragraph: yellow for the attention-getter and introductory comments, green for the thesis/focus sentence, and pink for the plan/sequence of main points.

3. Students will use the steps of the Structured Writing II process to plan, write, edit, and format an introductory paragraph.

4. Students will use the sequential editing steps in the Structured Writing process. They will use text-to-speech features to read and listen while checking the writing content, capitalization, punctuation, word usage, and spelling.

Materials Needed

Structured Writing II CD-ROM

- Introductory Paragraph Web
- Introductory Paragraph Organizer

Inspiration 6.0 or 7.0

Word processing program

Posters

- Introductory Paragraph Web

◆ Introductory Techniques and Attention-Getters

◆ Editing Steps (chapter 1)

Essential Elements

The Structured Writing II process teaches students to write an introductory paragraph containing:

1. An **attention-getter**

2. **Introductory comments**

3. A **thesis/focus sentence**

4. A **plan/sequence** of main points

Color Codes

◆ White for the essay title

◆ Blue for the paragraph type

◆ Yellow for attention-getter and introductory comments

◆ Green for thesis/focus sentence

◆ Pink for plan/sequence of main points

The Structured Writing II Process

Planning step: Outline the paragraph.

Writing step: Expand ideas into sentences. Organize sentences into a paragraph.

Editing step: Edit and revise the paragraph.

Formatting step: Create a draft.

Publishing step: Print the final copy. (Hold off on this step for now.)

The Editing Process

1. Open the organizer file.

2. Use text-to-speech to read and listen to each sentence, one at a time, to check content. Edit and revise.

3. Check capitalization.

4. Check punctuation.

5. Check for misused words (confusables/homonyms).

6. Run a spelling checker.

7. Read and listen to changes using text-to-speech.

8. Save changes.

9. Print in color or print and highlight by hand.

10. Give to a proofreader for review.

11. Make any necessary changes suggested by the proofreader.

12. Submit to the teacher for feedback and approval.

The Introductory Paragraph Process

The Planning Step

Students begin the planning step by opening the Inspiration template titled Introductory Paragraph Web. The template is on the CD-ROM accompanying this book. It is also reproduced in poster form on the following page. This template helps them organize their ideas for the introduction. The color code and the text identify the essential elements of this paragraph: **attention-getter** and **introductory**
comments, thesis/focus sentence, and the **plan/sequence of main points**. The introductory paragraph is not always the first paragraph to write in an essay. Many times the attention-getter and the introductory comments can be added after the rest of the essay is completed. Often, after the body paragraphs are written, it is easier to determine the most suitable introduction for the essay.

Introductory Paragraph Web

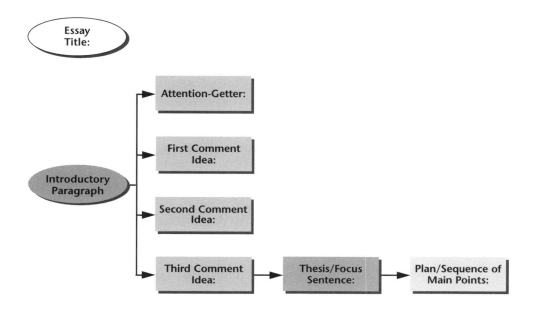

The following list provides directions for completing the planning step. Model the lesson using the topic "My Pets."

1. Students open the Introductory Paragraph Web. The white box in the web indicates the place for the essay title. The blue oval shows the paragraph type, or function. The yellow boxes are for an attention-getter and introductory comments. The green box is for the thesis/focus sentence. The pink box signifies the place for the overall plan or sequence of supporting ideas.

2. With the exception of the thesis/focus sentence, students type only single words and short phrases into the web to represent their ideas. Figure 3 shows the Introductory Paragraph Web with the pet ideas filled in. **Reinforce the distinction between organizing ideas by outlining and actually writing sentences.** The words and phrases will later be converted into an outline. The outline will be used to guide the creation of full sentences during the writing step using the Structured Writing II organizer template. Outlining ideas is a fundamental part of the writing process.

3. Students convert the web into a color-coded outline by selecting the Outline option in Inspiration. They should also use the software to check spelling to make initial corrections. Students save their outlines as "title.outline" in the appropriate folder or

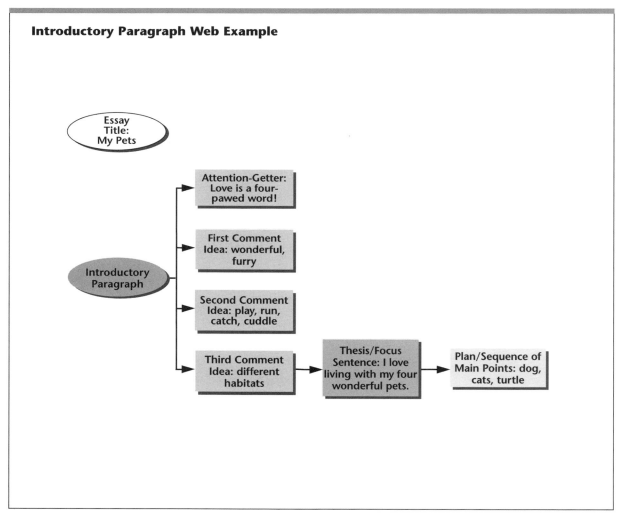

Introductory Paragraph Web Example

Figure 3. An Introductory Paragraph Web filled in with a student's ideas on pets.

Introductory Paragraph Outline	**Introductory Paragraph Outline**
Essay Title:	**Essay Title:** My Pets
A. Attention-Getter:	**A. Attention-Getter:** Love is a four-pawed word!
◆ *Ask a question.*	**B. First Comment:** wonderful, furry
◆ *Use a quotation, proverb, saying.*	**C. Second Comment:** play, run, catch, cuddle
◆ *Explain topic importance.*	**D. Third Comment:** different habitats
◆ *State opposite of point.*	1. Thesis/Focus Sentence: I love living with my four wonderful pets.
◆ *Provide a general statement/incident.*	a. Plan/Sequence of Main Points: dogs, cats, turtle
B. First Comment Idea:	
C. Second Comment Idea:	
D. Third Comment Idea:	
1. Thesis/Focus Sentence: *Main idea of the essay.*	
a. Plan/Sequence of Main Points:	

Figure 4. At left is the Introductory Paragraph Outline template. At right is the outline with the pet ideas filled in.

directory. Figure 4 shows the Introductory Paragraph Outline template and the Introductory Paragraph Outline with the pet ideas filled in.

4. Students print the color-coded outline or print it and highlight it by hand.

5. Students submit the outline to the teacher for review.

Teachers check the content and give the students feedback. Students use this outline to guide the next step of the process, the writing step.

The Writing Step

Students use the color-coded Introductory Paragraph Organizer and a word processing program (such as Write:OutLoud) as a guide to expand their ideas from the outline into complete sentences (Figure 5).

1. Using the outline as a guide, students create complete sentences in the organizer, one at a time. Each sentence will be revised later and edited in the editing step, sentence by sentence.

2. Students expand and elaborate their sentences as they write. They choose a **specific introduction technique** to get the reader's attention from the Introductory Techniques and Attention-Getters poster at the end of this chapter. Then they compose opening comments to further interest the reader and lead in to the main purpose of the essay.

Refer to the Introductory Techniques and Attention-Getters poster and try out various ways to get the reader's attention. Modeling a certain technique first and having students modify it using the other techniques provides good practice. This is a creative process and can be a wildly invigorating prewriting lesson. Be sure to have fun with it!

3. The **thesis/focus sentence** states the main point of the essay and must integrate a fact or facts with the writer's opinion or attitude about the topic. Students are encouraged to make the thesis/focus sentence forthright and exact.

4. The **plan reveals the sequence of supporting points** for the thesis/focus sentence that will make up the body paragraphs of the essay.

Introductory Paragraph Organizer	Example Introductory Paragraph Organizer
Essay Organizer by:	**Essay Organizer by:** Student Name
Essay Title:	**Essay Title:** My Pets
Attention-Getter:	**Attention-Getter:** Love is a four-pawed word!
First Comment:	**First Comment:** Animals are wonderful, furry beings that make great pets.
Second Comment:	**Second Comment:** Several animals like to play catch and chase.
Third Comment:	**Third Comment:** Many pets live in different habitats than people and are interesting to watch.
Thesis/Focus Sentence:	**Thesis/Focus Sentence:** I love living with my four wonderful pets.
Plan/Sequence of Main Points:	**Plan/Sequence of Main Points:** Sandy is my dog, Bert and Ernie are my cats, and Shelly is my box turtle.

Figure 5. At left is the Introductory Paragraph Organizer template. At right is the organizer with a student's sentences about pets.

5. Once all of the sentences are completed, the students save their Introductory Paragraph Organizers as "title.organizer" in the appropriate folder or directory.

6. Students print the organizers in color or print them and highlight them by hand for teacher review.

At this point, the teacher assesses the document for sentence structure and suggests ways to enhance the clarity and complexity of the writing.

The Editing Step

Students are required to use a specific editing sequence to make sure their sentences reflect their intended meaning and to correct spelling and mechanical errors. This step becomes more involved as the students move through the Structured Writing II process, with the number of paragraphs in a particular essay or report increasing along with the complexity of sentences and word choices. Encourage students to refer to the Editing Steps poster (chapter 1) to help them through the process.

1. Students open their saved organizer, "title.organizer."

2. Students use text-to-speech to read and listen to each sentence in their introductory paragraph, **one at a time.** Here, students check the content and add, delete, change, and rearrange words and sentences until they sound right and communicate their ideas.

◆ Students make sure they use an **effective attention-getter** and appropriate **introductory comments**. They make sure the **thesis/focus sentence** states the main idea of the essay and includes an opinion or attitude about the main idea.

◆ The **sequence of supporting ideas** is exposed in the plan. Students focus on various kinds of sentences (declarative, imperative, interrogative, exclamatory) and different types of sentences (simple, compound, complex) to elaborate and explain their thinking.

3. Students check capitalization (the beginning of each sentence and proper nouns, abbreviations, titles, and quotations).

4. Students check punctuation.

5. Students check word usage such as homonyms.

6. Students run the spelling checker in the word processor. When this step is performed after the other edits are made, it gives the students a better chance to properly correct misspelled words.

7. Students read and listen again to the changes they have made.

8. Students save their edited organizers as "title.organizer" in the appropriate folder or directory. This will replace the unedited version.

9. Students print their document in color or print it and highlight it by hand.

10. Students turn their document in to a proofreader for review. The proofreaders are other students in class who check for errors.

11. Students make any necessary changes suggested by the proofreader.

12. Students submit their documents to the teacher for inspection and approval.

The teacher assesses the sentences for structure, variation, and proper syntax to give feedback to the students. Reassured that content, syntax, grammar, structure, and spelling are correct, the students move to the formatting step.

The Formatting Step

In this step, students prepare the document for publishing. They remove the structure words from the Introductory Paragraph Organizer and put the sentences into paragraph format as a **draft**. The color code remains to reinforce the paragraph structure. Figure 6 shows an introductory paragraph that has been correctly formatted.

1. Students put the required heading on the document, such as their name and the date.

2. Students highlight the structure cues and delete them, one sentence at a time.

> Student Name
> Date
> ### My Pets
> Love is a four-pawed word! Animals are wonderful, furry beings that make great pets. Several animals like to play catch and chase. Many quadrupeds live in different habitats than people and are interesting to watch. I love living with my four wonderful pets. Sandy is my dog, Bert and Ernie are my cats, and Shelly is my box turtle.

Figure 6. A correctly formatted introductory paragraph.

"Structure cues" refers to the structure words in the organizer that identify the required elements (topic sentence, first supporting sentence, and so forth). As each cue is deleted, students arrange the sentences one after the other, paying close attention to beginning capitalization, ending punctuation, and spacing between sentences and lines.

3. Students center the title and indent the topic sentence.

4. Students read and listen again to the paragraph as a whole, assessing the flow and continuity of their ideas.

5. Students save their formatted paragraphs as "title.draft" in the appropriate folder or directory.

6. Students print the draft in color. If a color copier is not available, students use highlighters to identify the essential elements of the paragraph.

7. Students submit the draft to a proofreader for review.

The Publishing Step

At this point, when students receive approved drafts, the writing process is complete except for removing the color and printing a final copy. However, when writing essays and reports, the publishing step occurs after all the individual paragraphs have been formatted into one complete essay draft. Hold off on the publishing step for now. Once the entire draft has been proofread and approved, the essay is ready to be published.

Summary

In summary, the Introductory Paragraph Lesson introduces students to the essential elements of an opening paragraph for an essay or report:

1. An **attention-getter** as a topic sentence

2. **Introductory comments**

3. A **thesis/focus sentence** as the main idea

4. A **plan/sequence** of main points

Students must practice and master writing introductory paragraphs for essays. The thesis/focus sentences should sound more confident and decisive with experience. Teachers must be sure that students follow all the writing steps correctly to ensure accuracy and independence. Visual reminders (posters) displayed throughout the class and kept in student binders make a good reference. Specific practice in writing attention-getters and thesis/focus sentences is essential to good essay writing, and makes valuable a homework assignment.

The writing process is the same throughout this program. Students follow the same process for each paragraph within the essay. The planning step uses Inspiration and teacher-created templates. The writing step uses a word processing program and teacher-created organizers. The editing step follows the same sequence for all writing. The Structured Writing II process culminates with the formatting of individual paragraphs into the complete essay draft. The corrected draft is then published. While students will be asked to write various types of paragraphs and essays throughout the rest of this book, the Structured Writing II process and sequence remain the same.

Evaluation Rubric

The Introductory Paragraph Rubric focuses on student aptitude in following and filling out the paragraph organization and structure templates. It assesses their grasp of the fundamental mechanics of writing and the use of introductory techniques. The rubric is intended to aid teachers in evaluating the writing and to validate the writer.

Introductory Paragraph Rubric

STRUCTURE	EMERGING	DEVELOPING	PROFICIENT
Introductory Paragraph	Introductory paragraph contains: ◆ Thesis/focus sentence	Introductory paragraph contains: ◆ Thesis/focus sentence ◆ Plan/sequence of support topics	Introductory paragraph contains: ◆ Thesis/focus sentence ◆ Plan/sequence of support topics ◆ Introductory comments ◆ Attention-getter

MECHANICS	EMERGING	DEVELOPING	PROFICIENT
Capitalization	Correct capitalization of: ◆ Sentences	Correct capitalization of: ◆ Sentences ◆ Proper nouns	Correct capitalization of: ◆ Sentences ◆ Proper nouns ◆ Titles ◆ Quotations
Punctuation	Correct use of: ◆ Sentence-ending punctuation	Correct use of: ◆ Sentence-ending punctuation ◆ Quotation marks	Correct use of: ◆ Sentence-ending punctuation ◆ Quotation marks ◆ Commas ◆ Apostrophes
Spelling	Spelling is: ◆ Correct enough to read ◆ Inconsistently checked with spelling checker	Spelling is: ◆ Correct ◆ Effectively checked with spelling checker ◆ Checked with text-to-speech feature	Spelling is: ◆ Correct ◆ Effectively checked with spelling checker ◆ Checked with text-to-speech feature ◆ Correct for homonyms and proper nouns

Introductory Techniques and Attention-Getters!

▶ **Pose a Question**
Have you ever wondered how people get ideas for inventions?
Where in the world did Velcro come from?
Do you believe in superstitions?
What was life like before computers?

▶ **Ask a Question and Answer It**
Have you ever thrown a Halloween party? If you haven't, you should try it.
Do I get too much homework? You bet I do!
Should vending machines be allowed at schools? That depends on many things.
Is reality TV real? Get real!

▶ **Use a Quotation, Proverb, or Saying**
Henry Ford said, "Whether you think you can, or whether you think you can't, you're right!"
A picture is worth a thousand words.
So much homework, so little time.

▶ **Explain the Topic's Importance**
CPR training is essential for making schools safe.
Global warming is a worldwide concern.
You can change your behavior to become a successful student.
Computer literacy and keyboarding skills are required for school.

▶ **State the Opposite of the Point You Will Make**
Bees are only good for making honey.
School lunches must be good for students.
There isn't enough swoosh in the world!

▶ **Use an Anecdote (an Interesting or Funny Story)**
It was a long time ago that Johnny Benson started teasing me.
My first school dance was a disaster!
A dog named Fish can lead to misunderstandings.
If time means money, no wonder I'm broke!

▶ **Make a General Statement**
School uniforms are beneficial for students.
Many factors led to the American Revolution.
Muhammad Ali is the greatest boxer who ever lived.

Chapter 3

The Concluding Paragraph

Expository essays and reports require introductory and concluding paragraphs. In the introductory paragraph, writers come up with a main idea that announces the paper's theme. The purpose of the concluding paragraph is to recap the main points of the essay in a way that keeps the reader thinking about the topic while bringing it to an effective close. Writers start with a restatement of the thesis/focus sentence as a topic sentence. The main points are each summarized and commented upon. Finally, a clincher sentence leaves the reader with something to think about.

Students are encouraged to use many different concluding techniques to capture the reader's attention. These techniques (see the Possible Conclusions poster at the end of this chapter) allow students to effectively "wrap up" an essay or report in a variety of ways.

Objectives

1. Students will choose a specific method to construct a concluding paragraph, such as ask a question, give advice, or evaluate the evidence (see the Possible Conclusions poster at the end of this chapter).

2. Students will use the color codes to reinforce the essential elements of the concluding paragraph: yellow for a restatement of the thesis/focus sentence and the clincher sentence that wraps up the essay, green for sentences summarizing main points, pink for details.

3. Students will use the steps of the Structured Writing II process to plan, write, edit, and format a concluding paragraph.

4. Students will use the sequential editing steps in the Structured Writing process. They will use text-to-speech features to read and listen while checking the writing content, capitalization, punctuation, word usage, and spelling.

Materials Needed

Structured Writing II CD-ROM

- Concluding Paragraph Web
- Concluding Paragraph Organizer

Inspiration 6.0 or 7.0

Word processing program

Posters

- Concluding Paragraph Web
- Possible Conclusions
- Editing Steps (chapter 1)

Essential Elements

The Structured Writing II process teaches students to write a concluding paragraph using:

1. A **sentence that restates the thesis/focus sentence** in the introductory paragraph

2. **Three sentences supporting** each of the main points

3. **Details** to support each of the summary sentences

4. A **clincher sentence** to wrap up the essay

Color Codes

- White for the essay title
- Blue for the paragraph type
- Yellow for topic sentence and clincher sentence
- Green for supporting sentences
- Pink for details and elaboration

The Structured Writing II Process

Planning step: Outline the paragraph.

Writing step: Expand ideas into sentences. Organize sentences into a paragraph.

Editing step: Edit and revise the paragraph.

Formatting step: Create a draft.

Publishing step: Print the final copy. (Hold off on this step for now.)

The Editing Process

1. Open the organizer file.
2. Use text-to-speech to read and listen to each sentence, one at a time, to check content. Edit and revise.
3. Check capitalization.
4. Check punctuation.
5. Check for misused words (confusables/homonyms).
6. Run a spelling checker.
7. Read and listen to changes using text-to-speech.
8. Save changes.
9. Print in color or print and highlight by hand.
10. Give to a proofreader for review.
11. Make any necessary changes suggested by the proofreader.
12. Submit to the teacher for feedback and approval.

The Concluding Paragraph Process

The Planning Step

Students begin the planning step by opening the Inspiration template titled Concluding Paragraph Web. The template is on the CD-ROM accompanying this book. It is also reproduced in poster form on the following page. This will help them organize their thoughts and ideas for closing the essay in the concluding paragraph. The color code and text help identify the essential elements of the concluding paragraph: a **sentence restating the essay's thesis or focus** with a conclusion or fresh perspective on the thesis, **three sentences to summarize the main point of each supporting paragraph** in the essay, **details** and elaboration, and the **clincher sentence** (wrap-up).

Students refer to the Possible Conclusions poster at the end of this chapter to choose a method to close their essays. The Inspiration template also lists possible conclusions in the Notes feature for

Concluding Paragraph Web

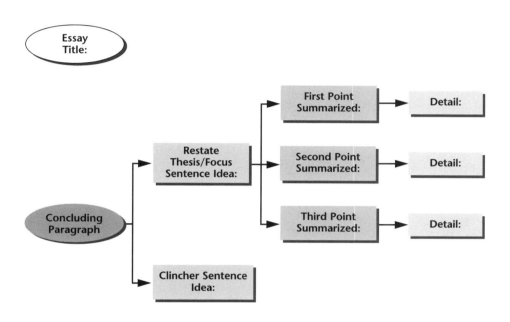

**Concluding Paragraph Outline
With Notes Showing**

Essay Title:

A. **Restate Thesis/Focus Sentence Idea:**
   - *State a new perspective/conclusion.*
   - *Echo focus sentence.*
   - *State lessons learned.*
   - *Give advice.*
   - *Question.*
   - *Summarize.*
   1. **First Point Summarized:** *Address essay's first point.*
      a. **Detail:**
   2. **Second Point Summarized:** *Address essay's second point.*
      a. **Detail:**
   3. **Third Point Summarized:** *Address essay's third point.*
      a. **Detail:**
B. **Clincher Sentence Idea:**
   - *Wish.*
   - *Exclamation.*
   - *Evaluation.*
   - *Future thought.*
   - *Another time/place.*
   - *Summary.*

**Concluding Paragraph Outline
With Notes Hidden**

Essay Title:

A. **Restate Thesis/Fous Sentence Idea:**
   1. **First Point Summarized:**
      a. **Detail:**
   2. **Second Point Summarized:**
      a. **Detail:**
   3. **Third Point Summarized:**
      a. **Detail:**
B. **Clincher Sentence Idea:**

Figure 7. Students should hide all notes before printing their outlines.

student reference. Students simply go to View in the main menu, select Notes, and click on Show All. The notes provide the cues for the various concluding techniques available to the students. It is best to show all notes as needed while composing. The example in Figure 7 shows the Concluding Paragraph Outline with the note cues showing and with them hidden.

Students must hide all notes before printing their outlines to simplify their presentation and avoid visual confusion. When the note scaffolding is no longer necessary, and before printing the outline, students go to View in the main menu, then Notes, and click on Hide All. Figure 8 illustrates how to hide notes in Inspiration.

When the notes are hidden and before printing, students go to File in the main menu, then Page

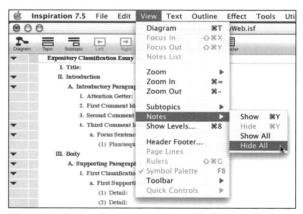

Figure 8. Go to the View menu to hide the notes on the outline.

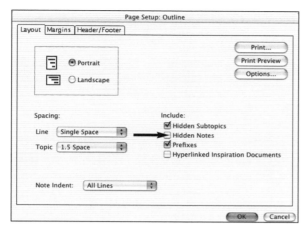

Figure 9. Use the Page Setup box to ensure that hidden notes do not print.

Setup to uncheck the box titled Hidden Notes. This keeps the notes on the color-coded outline from being printed. Figure 9 shows the location of the Hidden Notes box on Page Setup.

Once the Hidden Notes box is unchecked, students click OK to save the settings, or Print to print the color-coded outline immediately.

Teachers must point out the many possible conclusions that are feasible for an essay. The Possible Conclusions poster at the end of this chapter suggests several methods to use to close an essay. The following list provides directions for completing the planning step. Teachers can

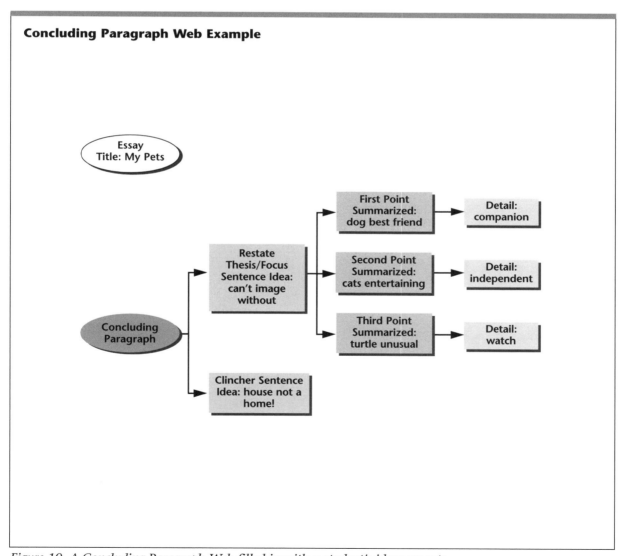

Figure 10. A Concluding Paragraph Web filled in with a student's ideas on pets.

Concluding Paragraph Outline

Essay Title:
A. **Restate Thesis/Focus Sentence Idea:**
   - *State a new perspective/conclusion.*
   - *Echo focus sentence.*
   - *State lessons learned.*
   - *Give advice.*
   - *Question.*
   - *Summarize.*
   1. **First Point Summarized:** *Address essay's first main point*
      a. **Detail:**
   2. **Second Point Summarized:** *Address essay's second main point*
      a. **Detail:**
   3. **Third Point Summarized:** *Address essay's thirrd main point*
      a. **Detail:**
B. **Clincher Sentence Idea:**
   - *Wish.*
   - *Exclamation.*
   - *Evaluation.*
   - *Future thought.*
   - *Another time/place.*
   - *Summary.*

Concluding Paragraph Outline

Essay Title: My Pets
A. **Restate Thesis/Focus Sentence Idea:** can't imagine without
   1. **First Point Summarized:** dog best friend
      a. **Detail:** companion
   2. **Second Point Summarized:** cats entertaining
      a. **Detail:** independent
   3. **Third Point Summarized:** turtle unusual
      a. **Detail:** watch
B. **Clincher Sentence Idea:** house not a home!

Figure 11. The outline at left shows notes that promote responses from students, such as those filled in at right.

model the various types of conclusions using the same topic as before, "My Pets."

1. Students open the Concluding Paragraph Web. The white box in the web indicates the place for the essay title; the blue oval shows the paragraph type, or function. The yellow boxes are for the topic sentence and the clincher sentence. The green boxes are for comments summarizing the supporting paragraphs, and the pink boxes are for details to enhance the author's specific feeling, attitude, or point of view.

2. With the exception of the thesis/focus sentence, students type key words and short phrases in the Concluding Paragraph Web to represent their ideas. **Reinforce the distinction between organizing ideas by outlining and actually writing sentences.** The key words and phrases will later be converted into an outline. The outline will be used as a guide to create complete sentences during the writing step using the Structured Writing II organizer template. Outlining ideas is a fundamental part of the writing process, especially when students are planning complex, multiple paragraph essays and reports. Figure 10 shows the Concluding Paragraph Web with the pet ideas filled in.

3. Students convert the web into a color-coded outline by selecting the Outline option in Inspiration. Here they can run an initial spelling check and easily rearrange their ideas. Students save the outline as "title.outline" in the appropriate folder or directory. Figure 11 shows the Concluding Paragraph Outline template and the Concluding Paragraph Outline with the pet ideas filled in.

4. When students are ready to print their outlines, they must first go to View in the main menu, then to Notes, and check Hide All to hide the notes on the outline. Then, students go to File in the main menu, scroll to Page Setup, and uncheck Hidden Notes. These procedures will keep the notes from appearing on the printed document.

5. Students print the color-coded outline or print it and highlight it by hand.

6. Students submit the outline for teacher review.

The teacher provides feedback on the student outlines. Reassured that they are on the right track, students use the outline to guide their efforts in the next step, the writing step.

The Writing Step

Students use the color-coded Concluding Paragraph Organizer and a word processing program to guide and expand their ideas from the outline into sentences in the organizer, one sentence at a time (Figure 12). The individual paragraphs are combined to form the essay, one edited paragraph at a time.

1. Using the outline as a guide, students compose complete sentences in the organizer, one sentence at a time. Each sentence will be revised later and edited in the editing step. The purpose here is to write one's thoughts without being distracted by writing mechanics or simultaneous mental editing.

2. Students expand and elaborate their sentences as they write. They select a particular method (see Possible Conclusions poster) to close their essays. Teachers direct students to use modifiers (adjectives, adverbs, prepositional phrases) to clarify their writing with strong verbs and specific nouns. They expand their writing by combining simple sentences into compound sentences, and varying the types (simple,

Concluding Paragraph Organizer

Essay Organizer by:

Essay Title:

Concluding Paragraph

Restate Thesis/Focus Sentence:

First Point Summarized:

Detail:

Second Point Summarized:

Detail:

Third Point Summarized:

Detail:

Clincher Sentence:

Example Concluding Paragraph Organizer

Essay Organizer by: Student Name

Essay Title: My Pets

Concluding Paragraph

Restate Thesis/Focus Sentence: I can't imagine living in a house without pets!

First Point Summarized: Dogs are truly man's best friends.

Detail: They make great companions.

Second Point Summarized: In addition, cats and their independent ways are quite entertaining.

Detail: They are warm and cuddly too.

Third Point Summarized: Box turtles and other "uncuddlies" are also extremely interesting to observe.

Detail: Nature provides lots of diversity among its beings.

Clincher Sentence: A house is not a home without animals!

Figure 12. At the organizer stage, students turn their ideas into complete sentences.

compound, complex) and kinds (declarative, imperative, interrogative, exclamatory) of sentences used.

3. When all the sentences in the concluding paragraph are completed, students save the organizer as "title.organizer" in the proper folder or directory.

Taking into account the student's level, the teacher assesses the document for sentence complexity and structure, paragraph content and structure, and successful use of closing comments and clincher sentences. Students should be encouraged and challenged to allow their personalities, perspectives, convictions, and humor to surface in their concluding paragraphs. If, however, bright ideas fail to materialize and no suitable conclusions occur to them, students can simply paraphrase the main points covered in the essay.

The Editing Step

Students are required to use the Structured Writing editing process for the essay's concluding paragraph to make sure the sentences and paragraph clearly reflect their ideas and to eliminate spelling and mechanical errors. It is best for students to learn a specific order to improve accuracy. This step becomes more elaborate as students proceed through the Structured Writing II sequence mainly because the complexity of the writing is increased. Encourage students to refer to the Editing Steps poster (chapter 1) to help them through the process.

1. Students open the file "title.organizer."

2. Students use text-to-speech to read and listen to each sentence in the concluding paragraph, one at a time, to check content. They add, delete, and change words until the sentences clearly express their intended meaning. Students edit and revise their concluding paragraphs one sentence at a time. This process helps the students to increase the complexity and clarity of their writing. Students vary the structure of their

sentences and use a thesaurus to build their vocabularies, eliminate overused words, and increase the sophistication of their writing.

3. Students check capitalization.

4. Students check punctuation.

5. Students check word usage, including homonyms and misused words.

6. Students check spelling. Using the spelling checker after the edits and revisions have been made gives the students a better chance to fix errors.

7. Students read and listen to changes using text-to-speech.

8. Students save their edited Concluding Paragraph Organizer as "title.organizer" in the proper folder or directory. This will replace the unedited organizer.

9. Students print the document in color or print it and highlight it by hand.

10. Students give the document to a proofreader for review.

11. Students make any necessary changes suggested by the proofreader.

12. Students submit the document to the teacher for feedback and approval.

It is best for teachers to assess a concluding paragraph for effect, relevant content, and appropriate structure individually with the student. Give suggestions for using various kinds of sentences and setting a particular tone to reassure students they are on the right track and to encourage and motivate them. Once you have reviewed the sentences with students, they are ready to format their concluding paragraphs.

The Formatting Step

In this step, students prepare the document for publishing. They remove the structure words from the organizer and put the sentences into individual paragraph form. The color code remains to reinforce the paragraph structure.

1. Students put the required heading on the document, such as their name, and identify the document as the concluding paragraph.

2. Students highlight the structure cues and delete them. As each structure cue is deleted, students arrange the sentences one after the other, paying attention to beginning capitalization and spacing after ending punctuation and between lines. Make sure that students know your spacing requirements: one or two spaces after ending punctuation, and single, one and a half, or double spacing between lines. It is also helpful to require a specific font and font size.

3. Students indent the topic sentence.

4. Students read and listen again to the essay's concluding paragraph as a whole, assessing the tone, flow, and continuity of ideas.

5. Students save the document as "title.draft" in the proper folder or directory.

6. Students print the draft in color or print it and highlight it by hand.

7. Students give the draft to a proofreader for review.

Initially, students practice using different methods to write concluding paragraphs for the same essay. They print out these paragraphs in color (or highlight them) to evaluate and assess them with their instructors. Figure 13 shows a concluding paragraph that has been correctly formatted.

When students become more experienced in writing essays using the Structured Writing II process, they will submit to a proofreader a draft of the whole essay (all color-coded drafts of individual paragraphs combined into essay form in one document labeled "essay title.draft").

The Publishing Step

The concluding paragraph does not go to the publishing step until it has been incorporated

---

Student Name

Date

Essay Title: **My Pets**

    I can't imagine living in a house without pets! Dogs are truly man's best friends. They make great companions. In addition, cats and their independent ways are quite entertaining. They are warm and cuddly too. Also, box turtles and other "uncuddlies" are extremely interesting to observe. Nature provides such wonderful diversity among its beings. A house is not a home without animals!

Figure 13. A correctly formatted concluding paragraph.

into the whole essay draft. After being proofread and revised, the whole essay draft is ready for the publishing step.

Summary

In summary, the essential elements of a closing paragraph for an essay or report include:

- A **sentence that restates the thesis/focus sentence** in the introductory paragraph

- **There sentences supporting** each of the main points

- **Details** to support each of the summary sentences

- A **clincher sentence** to wrap up the essay

The purpose of the concluding paragraph is to tie all the important points together and leave the reader with a clear idea of the essay's importance. It has two parts: a summary of the main points and a conclusion. It closes the essay after all the details have been included in the developmental paragraphs that make up the body of the essay. The suggested methods of closing an essay in the Possible Conclusions poster at the end of this chapter provide ways to enhance the tone, attitude, purpose, and perspective of the piece. All essays and reports must have a concluding paragraph.

Like the introductory paragraph, writing the concluding paragraph can be a very creative process, so try the different methods to demonstrate for students how to set a desired tone for an essay's closing. Sometimes writers use the writing process to clarify their thinking. If this is the case, a conclusion will often emerge at some point during the writing process. Other times, a writer's purpose is to prove a certain conviction, and his or her conclusion is clear from the beginning of the essay. When this is the case, the essay's concluding paragraph can be written before the introduction or body paragraphs. It is up to the individual teacher to determine when it is best to provide instruction on writing the conclusion. I prefer to teach my students to write the concluding paragraph after the body and introductory paragraphs have been designed.

Regardless of the order that each paragraph is written in the essay-writing process, each one is written separately, one sentence at a time. This allows students to focus on the paragraph's specific purpose and to choose the method, tone, and vocabulary appropriate to it. Encourage students to play with language and meaning: vary sentence structure, use punctuation to emphasize meaning, and mix up quotations to make a point or add humor. They can also just be blunt and make profound, introspective, or global observations. Modeling the various types of concluding paragraphs and showing how they should match the tone set in the essay's introductory paragraph provides students with examples and ideas to consider for their own compositions. Enjoy teaching and practicing this part of the essay. It's a unique way to empower students with their writing.

Students must master writing specialized introductory and concluding paragraphs before moving on to combine paragraphs into an essay. Learners experienced in the Structured Writing

process are now ready to combine the previously taught paragraph types into essays. They have experience writing reason, example, and process paragraphs that explain concepts using reasons, examples, or steps in a process. They understand how to structure classification and compare and contrast paragraphs using categories, similarities, and differences between things, and how to decide which particular paragraph type will best explain a theory or belief. They are now ready to stretch a paragraph into a five-paragraph essay.

Evaluation Rubric

The Concluding Paragraph Rubric focuses on student aptitude in following and filling out the paragraph organization and structure templates. It assesses their grasp of the fundamental mechanics of writing and the use of closing techniques. Teachers can use the rubric to evaluate the writing and validate the writer.

Concluding Paragraph Rubric

STRUCTURE	EMERGING	DEVELOPING	PROFICIENT
Concluding Paragraph	Concluding paragraph contains: ◆ Reference to thesis/focus sentence	Concluding paragraph contains: ◆ Reference to thesis/focus sentence ◆ Summary of support topics	Concluding paragraph contains: ◆ Reference to thesis/focus sentence ◆ Summary of support topics ◆ Effective closing techniques

MECHANICS	EMERGING	DEVELOPING	PROFICIENT
Capitalization	Correct capitalization of: ◆ Sentences	Correct capitalization of: ◆ Sentences ◆ Proper nouns	Correct capitalization of: ◆ Sentences ◆ Proper nouns ◆ Titles ◆ Quotations
Punctuation	Correct use of: ◆ Sentence-ending punctuation	Correct use of: ◆ Sentence-ending punctuation ◆ Quotation marks	Correct use of: ◆ Sentence-ending punctuation ◆ Quotation marks ◆ Commas ◆ Apostrophes
Spelling	Spelling is: ◆ Correct enough to read ◆ Inconsistently checked with spelling checker	Spelling is: ◆ Correct ◆ Effectively checked with spelling checker ◆ Checked with text-to-speech feature	Spelling is: ◆ Correct ◆ Effectively checked with spelling checker ◆ Checked with text-to-speech feature ◆ Correct for homonyms and proper nouns

Possible Conclusions

▶ **Advice for the Reader**
Never again will I go to a rock concert without earplugs.
Be careful what you wish for.

▶ **A Question**
Do you think bees are more important now?
Is America changing its national game?

▶ **An Evaluation**
Studying smarter makes more sense than studying harder.
America's demand for fresh water is approaching nature's limits.

▶ **Lessons Learned**
If it looks too good to be true, it probably isn't true.
Honesty is the best policy!

▶ **Future Thoughts**
I can hardly wait until I am old enough to drive.
Will there be any elephants left in the world for my children to see?

▶ **Another Place and Time**
In Japan, children go to school six days a week.
Fifty years from now, technology will be very different.

▶ **A Suggested Course of Action**
If you want to succeed in school, do your homework.
Everybody who is good at anything got that way by working.

▶ **A Wish**
If only I were taller.
I wish the world were rid of homelessness.

▶ **A Strong Image**
Smiling children with grenades hidden in their pockets haunt my dreams.
New York will always be a city with two burning towers in my mind.

▶ **A Bit of Wit**
Got milk?
Have a Coke and a smile!

Chapter 4

Paragraph to Essay

After students have learned to write the various expository paragraphs described in *Structured Writing* and have composed several introductory and concluding paragraphs, they are ready to stretch a paragraph into an essay. The first and most important step is to show students how the structural elements of a paragraph compare with the corresponding elements of a longer essay. The topic sentence of the paragraph becomes the thesis/focus sentence in the introductory paragraph of the essay. The three supporting sentences in the paragraph are stretched and elaborated into three individual supporting paragraphs in the essay. The concluding sentence of the paragraph is, in turn, expanded into a concluding paragraph in the essay. By emphasizing this structural similarity and building on familiar concepts, you can persuade students of their ability to write a full essay, one paragraph at a time.

When teaching students how to "stretch" a paragraph into an essay, it is sometimes best to write the entire introductory paragraph after the body paragraphs have been composed. The thesis/focus sentence needs to be set, but the introductory comments and attention-getter can be easier to compose after the rest of the essay is completed. Sometimes when students begin elaborating the body paragraphs, sweeping statements and generalizations about the topic become more numerous. These general statements can be used as introductory comments or may spark the use of a specific technique to use in the introductory paragraph.

However, sometimes writing the concluding paragraph first is appropriate, especially when students are writing persuasive essays. Students can initially write a concluding paragraph and then prepare the various body paragraphs to either deductively, inductively, or chronologically establish their perspective. Alerting students to the types of decisions they will need to consider when writing essays is crucial and efficiently taught by modeling.

Objectives

1. Students will expand a basic paragraph into a five-paragraph essay using an introductory paragraph, three supporting paragraphs, and a concluding paragraph.

2. Students will use the steps of the Structured Writing II process to plan, write, edit, format, and publish a five-paragraph essay.

3. Students will use the sequential editing steps in the Structured Writing process. They will use text-to-speech features to read and listen while checking the writing content, capitalization, punctuation, word usage, and spelling. They will make revisions to increase sentence complexity and use a thesaurus to enhance vocabulary and eliminate overused words.

Materials Needed

Structured Writing II CD-ROM

- Essay Web
- Essay Organizer

Inspiration 6.0 or 7.0

Word processing program

Posters

- Essay Web
- Suggested Topics for Paragraph to Essay
- Five-Paragraph Essay Planner
- Editing Steps (chapter 1)
- Possible Conclusions (chapter 3)

Essential Elements

The Structured Writing II process teaches students to write a five-paragraph essay using:

1. An **introductory paragraph**
2. **Three supporting paragraphs** with **transition sentences**
3. A **concluding paragraph**

Color Codes

- White for the essay title
- Blue for paragraph types
- Yellow for topic and concluding sentences
- Green for supporting sentences
- Pink for details and elaboration

The Structured Writing II Process

Planning step: Outline the essay.

Writing step: Expand ideas into sentences. Organize sentences in paragraphs.

Editing step: Edit and revise one paragraph at a time.

Formatting step: Create a draft in essay format.

Publishing step: Print the final copy.

The Editing Process

1. Open the organizer file.
2. Use text-to-speech to read and listen to each sentence, one at a time, to check content. Edit and revise.
3. Check capitalization.
4. Check punctuation.
5. Check for homonyms and misused words.
6. Run a spelling checker.
7. Read and listen to changes using text-to-speech.
8. Save changes.
9. Print in color or print and highlight by hand.
10. Submit to a proofreader for review.
11. Make any necessary changes suggested by the proofreader.
12. Give to the teacher for feedback and approval.

The Paragraph to Essay Process

The Planning Step

Students begin the planning step by opening the Inspiration template Essay Web. The template is on the CD-ROM accompanying this book. It is also reproduced in poster form on the page 39. This template helps students plan the essay before writing it. The color code and text identify the essential parts of the essay (title, introductory paragraph, three supporting paragraphs, and concluding paragraph), and the essential elements of each paragraph (topic sentence, supporting sentences, and concluding sentence).

Teachers can model the lesson using the essay topic "My Pets." Students can refer to the basic paragraph "My Pets" from Structured Writing (Figure 14), and see how it can be expanded into a five-paragraph essay.

The topic sentence of the basic paragraph becomes the thesis/focus sentence in the introductory paragraph, the three supporting sentences are each expanded into separate paragraphs that make up the body of the essay, and the concluding sentence becomes the closing thought for the concluding paragraph. For help with generating essay ideas, refer to the Suggested Topics for Paragraph to Essay poster. The Five-Paragraph Essay Planner poster provides an outline for guidance through the planning process. Both posters are located at

the end of this chapter. The following list provides directions for completing the planning step.

1. Students open the Essay Web. The white box in the web indicates the place for the essay title. The blue ovals identify the paragraph types, or functions, within the essay. The yellow boxes are for topic and concluding sentence ideas within each paragraph. The green boxes signify the places for supporting sentence ideas. The pink boxes are for the details about the supporting ideas.

2. With the exception of the thesis/focus sentence, students type key words and short phrases in the web to represent their ideas. (The foldout page in this chapter shows the Essay Web on one side and the Essay Web with the pet ideas filled in on the other side.) **Reinforce the distinction between developing and organizing ideas by outlining and actually writing sentences.** It is important that students organize their ideas for the essay as a whole before starting to write. The type and order of the essay's body paragraphs will depend on the purpose of the essay. It is best to make this determination in the planning step. The words and phrases will then be converted into an outline to use as a guide for writing each paragraph later in the writing step.

3. When all the boxes have been filled in, students convert the web into a color-coded outline by selecting the Outline option in Inspiration. If changes need to be made in the order of the paragraphs, it is easier to rearrange them in the outline format. Students run the spelling checker and save the Essay Outline as "essay title.outline" in the appropriate folder or directory. Figure 15 shows how the Essay Outline appears on the computer screen.

Student Name

Date

My Pets

I have four pets. My dog is named Sandy. I have two cats, Bert and Ernie. My box turtle lives in a heated aquarium in my room. I love my pets.

Figure 14. An example of a Basic Paragraph.

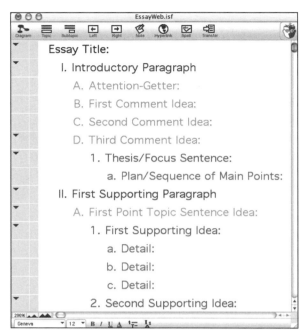

Figure 15. A partial Essay Outline on the computer screen.

4. Some students may be overwhelmed or distracted by the whole essay while working on individual paragraphs. To simplify the visuals, close the topic windows in the Inspiration outline format and let students view only one paragraph at a time while they write (see Figure 16).

5. When students are ready to print their outlines, they must first go to View in the main menu, then to Notes, and check Hide All to hide the notes on the outline. Then, students go to File in the main menu, scroll to Page Setup, and uncheck Hidden Notes (see chapter 3 for more information). These steps will keep the notes from appearing on the printed document.

6. Students print the color-coded outline or print it and highlight it by hand.

7. Students submit the outline to the teacher for review.

The teacher checks for content, order, and completeness to give feedback to the students before they begin the writing step. Reassured that they are on the right track, students use the outline to guide their efforts when writing.

The Writing Step

Writing an essay one paragraph at a time breaks the process into manageable bites. Teachers must customize the process to fit instructional time restraints and accommodate student needs. The typical 45-minute instructional period is sometimes too long or too short for a particular aspect of the Structured Writing II process or for the needs of individual students. I typically use the first period to provide an overview of the writing process, building in a review of skills and a time for practice for the class as a whole. This allows me to assess the writing skill and experience of the individual students. During the second instructional period, I generally model one or more steps in the writing process for a particular essay assignment, using a class monitor and encouraging direct student involvement. When modeling, I act as a secretary taking dictation while the students do all the thinking and composing.

Once the entire essay has been modeled from outline to final copy, I assign the same topic for students to work on individually. The time it takes for students to complete each of the separate steps in the writing process is dependent on individual attention spans and writing levels. Those with shorter attention spans can use the completion of steps within individual paragraphs as mini-goals and places to take breaks. Be sure to guarantee success—make sure that students leave each class period with a sense of accomplishment. If you have limited instructional time, match your instruction to that time. Teaching the process to inexperienced or struggling writers is time-consuming. However, direct instruction of these sequential steps is necessary to provide students with the structure and organization they need to improve their writing.

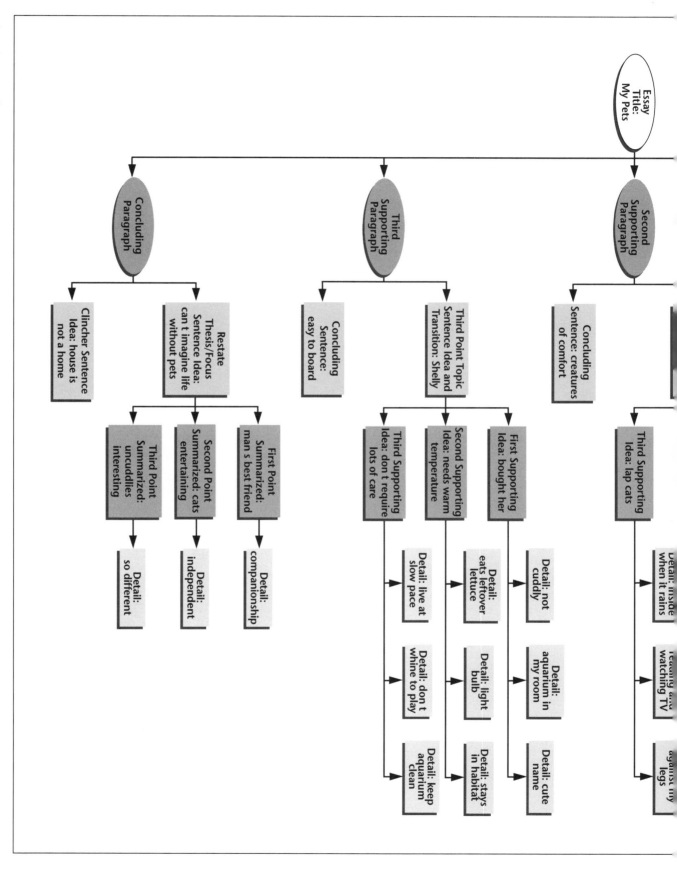

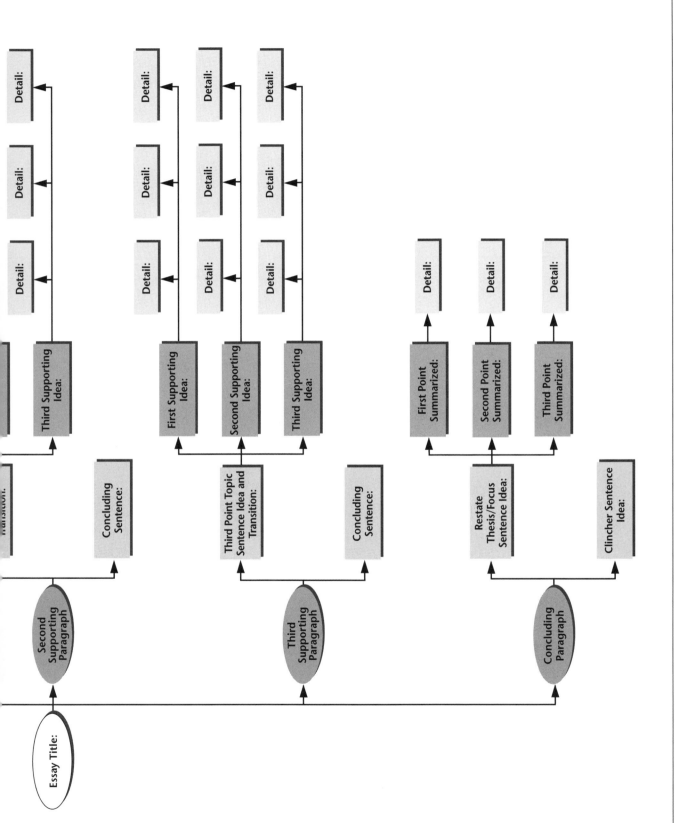

Essay Web

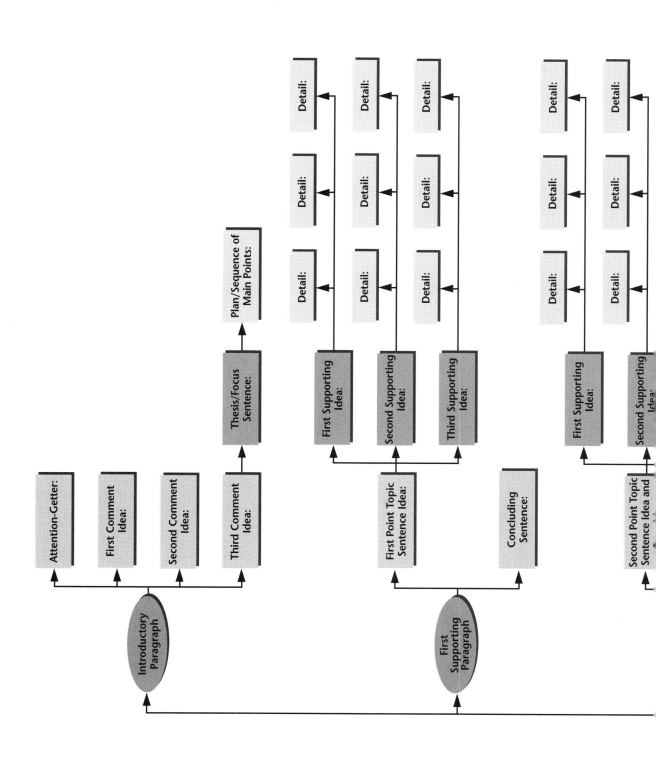

Attention-Getter:

First Comment Idea:

Second Comment Idea:

Third Comment Idea:

Thesis/Focus Sentence:

Plan/Sequence of Main Points:

Introductory Paragraph

First Point Topic Sentence Idea:

Concluding Sentence:

First Supporting Paragraph

First Supporting Idea:

Second Supporting Idea:

Third Supporting Idea:

Detail: Detail: Detail:

Detail: Detail: Detail:

Detail: Detail: Detail:

Second Point Topic Sentence Idea and

First Supporting Idea:

Second Supporting Idea:

Detail: Detail: Detail:

Detail: Detail: Detail:

Essay Web Example

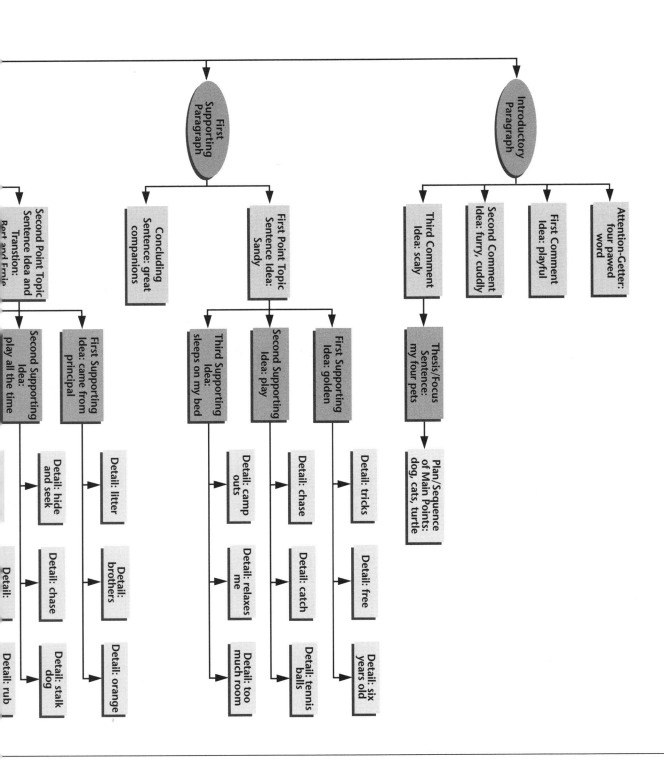

Introductory Paragraph
- Attention-Getter: four pawed word
- First Comment Idea: playful
- Second Comment Idea: furry, cuddly
- Third Comment Idea: scaly
  - Thesis/Focus Sentence: my four pets
    - Plan/Sequence of Main Points: dog, cats, turtle

First Supporting Paragraph
- Concluding Sentence: great companions
- First Point Topic Sentence Idea: Sandy
  - First Supporting Idea: golden
    - Detail: tricks
    - Detail: free
    - Detail: six years old
  - Second Supporting Idea: play
    - Detail: chase
    - Detail: catch
    - Detail: tennis balls
  - Third Supporting Idea: sleeps on my bed
    - Detail: camp outs
    - Detail: relaxes me
    - Detail: too much room
- Second Point Topic Sentence Idea and Transition: Bert and Ernie
  - First Supporting Idea: came from principal
    - Detail: litter
    - Detail: brothers
    - Detail: orange
  - Second Supporting Idea: play all the time
    - Detail: hide and seek
    - Detail: chase
    - Detail: stalk dog
    - Detail:
    - Detail: rub

Essay Outline

Essay Title:

I. Introductory Paragraph
   A. Attention-Getter:
   B. First Comment Idea:
   C. Second Comment Idea:
   D. Third Comment Idea:
      1. Thesis/Focus Sentence:
         a. Plan/Sequence of Main Points:

II. First Supporting Paragraph
   A. First Point Topic Sentence Idea:
      1. First Supporting Idea:
         a. Detail:
         b. Detail:
         c. Detail:
      2. Second Supporting Idea:
         a. Detail:
         b. Detail:
         c. Detail:
      3. Third Supporting Idea:
         a. Detail:
         b. Detail:
         c. Detail:
   B. Concluding Sentence:

III. Second Supporting Paragraph
   A. Second Point Topic Sentence Idea and Transition:
      1. First Supporting Idea:
         a. Detail:
         b. Detail:
         c. Detail:
      2. Second Supporting Idea:
         a. Detail:

b. Detail:
c. Detail:
      3. Third Supporting Idea:
         a. Detail:
         b. Detail:
         c. Detail:
   B. Concluding Sentence:

IV. Third Supporting Paragraph
   A. Third Point Topic Sentence Idea and Transition:
      1. First Supporting Idea:
         a. Detail:
         b. Detail:
         c. Detail:
      2. Second Supporting Idea:
         a. Detail:
         b. Detail:
         c. Detail:
      3. Third Supporting Idea:
         a. Detail:
         b. Detail:
         c. Detail:
   B. Concluding Sentence:

V. Concluding Paragraph
   A. Restate Thesis/Focus Sentence Idea:
      1. First Point Summarized:
         a. Detail:
      2. Second Point Summarized:
         a. Detail:
      3. Third Point Summarized:
         a. Detail:
   B. Clincher Sentence Idea:

Essay Outline With Only Introductory Paragraph Details Showing

Essay Title:

I. Introductory Paragraph
   A. Attention-Getter:
   B. First Comment Idea:
   C. Second Comment Idea:
   D. Third Comment Idea:
      1. Thesis/Focus Sentence:
         a. Plan/Sequence of Main Points:

II. First Supporting Paragraph

III. Second Supporting Paragraph

IV. Third Supporting Paragraph

V. Concluding Paragraph

Figure 16. At top is the Essay Outline template in full detail. At bottom is the Essay Outline template with only the introductory paragraph displayed in detail.

Compose the Supporting Paragraphs

To expand a paragraph into an essay, students will begin with the three supporting, or body, paragraphs, one at a time, and then write the introductory paragraph and concluding paragraph separately. Students use the color-coded Structured Writing Essay Organizer (Figure 17) and word processing program to guide and expand their ideas from the outline into complete sentences in the individual paragraph organizers, one paragraph at a time.

1. When beginning to write the body paragraphs, students start with the topic sentence for the first body paragraph. They

---

Essay Organizer

Essay Organizer by:
Essay Title:

Introductory Paragraph
    Attention-Getter:
    First Comment:
    Second Comment:
    Third Comment:
    Thesis/Focus Sentence:
    Plan/Sequence of Main Points:

First Supporting Paragraph
    Topic Sentence:
    First Supporting Sentence:
    Detail:
    Detail:
    Detail:
    Second Supporting Sentence:
    Detail:
    Detail:
    Detail:
    Third Supporting Sentence:
    Detail:
    Detail:
    Detail:
    Concluding Sentence:

Second Supporting Paragraph
    Topic Sentence and Transition:
    First Supporting Sentence:
    Detail:
    Detail:
    Detail:
    Second Supporting Sentence:
    Detail:

    Detail:
    Detail:
    Third Supporting Sentence:
    Detail:
    Detail:
    Detail:
    Concluding Sentence:

Third Supporting Paragraph
    Topic Sentence and Transition:
    First Supporting Sentence:
    Detail:
    Detail:
    Detail:
    Second Supporting Sentence:
    Detail:
    Detail:
    Detail:
    Third Supporting Sentence:
    Detail:
    Detail:
    Detail:
    Concluding Sentence:

Concluding Paragraph
    Restate Thesis/Focus Sentence:
    First Point Summarized:
    Detail:
    Second Point Summarized:
    Detail:
    Third Point Summarized:
    Detail:
    Clincher Sentence:

Figure 17. The complete five-paragraph Essay Organizer template.

use the first supporting sentence from the basic paragraph "My Pets" as the topic sentence for the first supporting paragraph in the essay. The supporting sentence in the basic paragraph, "I have a dog named Sandy," is expanded to "My dog, Sandy, is my favorite pet," the topic sentence for the first body paragraph in this essay. Students learn to follow the outline to compose the essay, one paragraph at a time, elaborating and writing supporting and detail sentences. They make sure sentences are complete and clearly express their intended meaning (Figure 18). Each paragraph will be edited and revised in the editing step.

2. Students are alerted to the second supporting sentence from the basic paragraph, "I have two cats, Bert and Ernie," and see how it is expanded into the topic sentence for the second supporting paragraph. Students follow the model and elaborate the sentences in the writing step.

◆ Encourage students to use adjective and adverb modifiers and prepositional phrases to clarify their prose.

◆ Prompt students to combine simple sentences into compound sentences, to use complex sentences, and to vary sentence structure.

◆ Encourage students to consult a thesaurus to eliminate overused words, improve vocabulary, and enhance the intricacy of their written expression.

◆ Remind students to use appropriate transition words in the green structure sentences to indicate the main points within each paragraph.

3. Once the sentences in the first supporting paragraph are completed, students save it as "essay title.organizer" in the proper folder or directory. They then move on to the second supporting paragraph, and then the third. Each subsequent paragraph will

---

Example Essay Organizer—Introductory Paragraph and First Supporting Paragraph

Essay Organizer by: Student Name
Essay Title: My Pets

Introductory Paragraph

  Attention-Getter:

  First Comment:

  Second Comment:

  Third Comment:

  Thesis/Focus Sentence: I love living with my four wonderful pets.

  Plan/Sequence of Main Points: Sandy is my dog, Bert and Ernie are my cats, and Shelly is my box turtle.

First Supporting Paragraph

  Topic Sentence: My dog, Sandy, is my favorite pet.

  First Supporting Sentence: Sandy is a Golden Retriever.

  Detail: Mom saw an advertisement in the newspaper that said Sandy was free to a good home, so Mom unexpectedly brought her home one afternoon.

  Detail: Sandy is six years old and very smart.

  Detail: She is well mannered and trained to do several tricks.

  Second Supporting Sentence: Also, Sandy loves to play.

  Detail: She especially likes to play catch with tennis balls.

  Detail: She does a funny trick while lying on her back with three tennis balls balanced on her front feet.

  Detail: She is always ready for a game of chase, too!

  Third Supporting Sentence: In addition, Sandy sleeps on my bed at night.

  Detail: She keeps me company and relaxes me.

  Detail: Sometimes she takes up too much room on the bed.

  Detail: On summer nights, she sleeps in the tent with me in the backyard.

  Concluding Sentence: Dogs are terrific companions.

Figure 18. A partially filled in organizer.

be added to the Essay Organizer when students save what they have completed as "essay title.organizer." (The entire Essay Organizer will be arranged into a draft in the formatting step.)

Students write one supporting paragraph at a time, one sentence at a time. Each paragraph is treated as a separate entity within the whole document to ensure continuity and improve accuracy. **Focus is placed on the concept of transition sentences as topic sentences that unite the separate sections within the essay.**

Transitions

Teachers teach one new concept in the Paragraph to Essay Lesson: using **transition sentences** to connect the supporting paragraphs within the essay. Topic sentences link with the previous paragraph to keep the flow of ideas smooth between paragraphs. The Structured Writing II process teaches the use of transition words and phrases in the topic sentences of the second and third supporting paragraphs. Generating and posting examples of transition sentences helps students to use them with confidence.

Transition sentences combine the ideas from the first supporting paragraph and the second supporting paragraph into a topic sentence that links the two paragraphs together. Likewise, a transition sentence that includes the main ideas from each of the preceding supporting paragraphs becomes the topic sentence for the third supporting paragraph and maintains the smooth flow of ideas (Figure 19).

Compose the Introductory Paragraph

Once the body paragraphs are complete, students attend to the introductory paragraph. Using the topic sentence from the basic paragraph as the thesis/focus sentence, students try various introduction techniques to get their reader's attention and open the essay. They

develop the attention-getter using related comments and details to "hook" the reader. This paragraph's concluding sentence reveals the order of the supporting paragraphs to follow.

Teachers focus on the essential elements of the introductory paragraph: an attention-getter, introductory comments, a thesis/focus sentence, and a plan/sequence of supporting paragraphs.

Following the Structured Writing II process, students use the introductory paragraph section in the Essay Organizer to expand their ideas into sentences, one at a time. Text cues indicate the appropriate information, and the color code reinforces the paragraph structure. Teachers direct students to take into account the purpose of their essays and the tone of the opening, choosing colorful adjectives and strong verbs to "hook" the reader. (See chapter 2, the Introductory Paragraph Lesson, for more details.)

When the introductory paragraph sentences are finished, the students save it as "essay title.organizer" in the proper folder or directory (thereby adding the introductory paragraph to the three supporting paragraphs that are already in the organizer). They then move on to the concluding paragraph.

Compose the Concluding Paragraph

Teachers focus on the essential elements of the concluding paragraph: a topic sentence restating the thesis/focus sentence (from the introductory paragraph) using a specific method (see the Possible Conclusions poster at the end of chapter 3), three supporting sentences summarizing each of the three body paragraphs, one or more details about each, and a clincher sentence.

Students use the concluding paragraph section in the Essay Organizer to expand their closing ideas into sentences, one at a time. Structure cues indicate the required information, and the color code reinforces the paragraph structure.

- Teachers encourage students to take a stand when deciding how to end their essays. Students consider the audience and purpose for writing the essay, the tone they have established, and the points made to determine a memorable conclusion.

- Students answer any questions unanswered in the supporting paragraphs, summarize the main points, or emphasize the special importance of one of the main points.

- Concluding paragraphs restate the thesis/focus sentence and say something that will keep the readers thinking about the subject. Leaving readers with a strong image, or perhaps a bit of wit, effectively "wraps up" a composition. (See chapter 3, the Concluding Paragraph Lesson.)

When the concluding paragraph is complete, students save it as "essay title.organizer" in the proper folder or directory (adding it to the three supporting paragraphs and introductory paragraph already in the organizer).

Example Transition Sentence Linking First and Second Supporting Paragraphs

Second Supporting Paragraph

Topic Sentence and Transition: *Along with my dog, Sandy, I have two cats, Bert and Ernie.*

First Supporting Sentence: Initially, they belonged to the principal at my school.

Detail: Mr. Alexander's cat had kittens, and he needed to find good homes for them.

Detail: Bert and Ernie are brothers from that litter.

Detail: Both have orange fur with white stripes and look exactly alike.

Second Supporting Sentence: Bert and Ernie love to play, too.

Detail: They chase each other, their tails, string, and nearly anything that moves.

Detail: They stalk Sandy and pounce on paper bags.

Detail: They run after dust balls and play hide and seek with each other.

Third Supporting Sentence: Finally, cats will often curl up in a warm lap.

Detail: Bert snuggles and likes to curl up in my lap when I'm reading or watching TV.

Detail: Ernie prefers to rub against my legs.

Detail: On cold, rainy evenings both felines can be found in a warm, cozy spot.

Concluding Sentence: Cats are independent creatures of comfort.

Example Transition Sentence Linking Second and Third Supporting Paragraphs

Third Supporting Paragraph

Topic Sentence and Transition: *In addition to my dog and cats, I also have a box turtle named Shelly.*

First Supporting Sentence: One day she caught my eye at the pet store, so I used my allowance to buy her.

Detail: She lives in a lighted aquarium in my bedroom.

Detail: I named her Shelly because of her big shell.

Detail: She is very interesting to watch and definitely is not cuddly!

Second Supporting Sentence: Also, box turtles need warm temperatures.

Detail: The light in her aquarium keeps her body temperature constant.

Detail: Shelly likes to stay in her habitat but will walk around on my rug on warm days sometimes.

Detail: She eats leftover lettuce and vegetables.

Third Supporting Sentence: Most important, box turtles don't require as much attention as dogs or cats.

Detail: They don't whine to play with you.

Detail: You have to keep their aquariums clean, but you don't have to feed them every day.

Detail: Turtles move at a slow pace and encourage me to slow down.

Concluding Sentence: Turtles are out of the ordinary and fun to watch.

Figure 19. Examples of transition sentences are underlined and italicized.

The Editing Step

Students edit one paragraph at a time within the Essay Organizer using the Structured Writing process. Students check capitalization, punctuation, word usage, and spelling in the specific order described in the Structured Writing editing process. Encourage students to refer to the Editing Steps poster (chapter 1) to help them through the process.

1. Students open their saved organizer, "essay title.organizer."

2. Students read and listen to each paragraph, one sentence at a time, using the text-to-speech feature to check the content of their writing beginning with the introductory paragraph. Each separate paragraph is edited and revised as a whole within the entire multi-paragraph essay.

   ◆ Students add, delete, rearrange, and change words until the sentences sound "right" and communicate the intended meaning.

   ◆ Students focus on refining the essay. They practice varying the sentence structure, using different kinds of sentences, and consult a thesaurus to eliminate overused words and increase the complexity of the vocabulary.

3. Students check capitalization.

4. Students check punctuation.

5. Students check word usage, including homonyms and misused words.

6. Students check spelling.

7. Students read and listen to changes using text-to-speech.

8. Students save the edited organizer as "essay title.organizer" in the proper folder or directory. This will replace the unedited organizer.

9. Students print the Essay Organizer in color or print it and highlight it by hand.

10. Students submit the document to a proofreader for review.

11. Students make any necessary changes suggested by the proofreader.

12. Students give the document to the teacher for inspection and approval.

Teachers assess the sentences and paragraphs in the organizer for appropriate content, proper syntax, and sentence variation. Once edited organizers are approved, students move to the formatting step.

At this point, students have edited the individual paragraph organizers within the essay, one at a time. These paragraphs have been saved in the essay folder and are now ready to be formatted into the complete essay and saved as a new document.

The Formatting Step

In the formatting step, students prepare the document for publishing. They put the paragraphs from the organizer into essay form, removing the structure cues, centering the title, indenting topic sentences, and checking appropriate spacing after ending punctuation. The color code remains to reinforce paragraph structure within the essay.

1. Students put the required heading on the document, such as their name and the date.

2. Students delete the structure words and place the sentences in proper paragraph form, one paragraph at a time, beginning with the introductory paragraph. Students maintain appropriate spacing after ending punctuation (one or two spaces) and between lines (single, one and a half, or double spacing). The same procedure is used for each of the remaining paragraphs.

3. Students center the essay title and indent topic sentences.

4. Students read and listen to the entire essay, paying attention to the flow of ideas.

Student Name

Date

My Pets

Love is a four-pawed word! Animals are amazing beings and make great pets. Several animals like to play catch and chase. Others are furry and like to cuddle, while some are just plain fun to watch. I love living with my four wonderful pets. Sandy is my dog, Bert and Ernie are my cats, and Shelly is my box turtle.

My dog, Sandy, is my favorite pet. Sandy is a Golden Retriever. Mom saw an advertisement in the newspaper that said Sandy was free to a good home, so Mom unexpectedly brought her home one afternoon. Sandy is six years old and very smart. She is well mannered and trained to do several tricks. Also, Sandy loves to play. She especially likes to play catch with tennis balls. She does a funny trick while lying on her back with three tennis balls balanced on her front feet. She is always ready for a game of chase, too! In addition, Sandy sleeps on my bed at night. She keeps me company and relaxes me. Sometimes she takes up too much room on the bed. On summer nights, she sleeps in the tent with me in the backyard. Dogs are terrific companions.

Along with my dog, Sandy, I have two cats, Bert and Ernie. Initially, they belonged to the principal at my school. Mr. Alexander's cat had kittens, and he needed to find good homes for them. Bert and Ernie are brothers from that litter. Both have orange fur with white stripes and look exactly alike. Bert and Ernie love to play, too. They chase each other, their tails, string, and nearly anything that moves. They stalk Sandy and pounce on paper bags. They run after dust balls and play hide and seek with each other. Finally, cats will often curl up in a warm lap. Bert snuggles and likes to curl up in my lap when I'm reading or watching TV. Ernie prefers to rub against my legs. On cold, rainy evenings both felines can be found in a warm, cozy spot. Cats are independent creatures of comfort.

In addition to my dog and cats, I also have a box turtle named Shelly. One day she caught my eye at the pet store, so I used my allowance to buy her. She lives in a lighted aquarium in my bedroom. I named her Shelly because of her big shell. She is very interesting to watch and definitely is not cuddly! Also, box turtles need warm temperatures. The light in her aquarium keeps her body temperature constant. Shelly likes to stay in her habitat but will walk around on my rug on warm days sometimes. She eats leftover lettuce and vegetables. Most important, box turtles don't require as much attention as dogs or cats. They don't whine to play with you. You have to keep their aquariums clean, but you don't have to feed them every day. Turtles move at a slow pace and encourage me to slow down. Turtles are out of the ordinary and fun to watch.

I can't imagine living in a home without animals! Dogs truly are man's best friends. They make excellent companions. Cats are amusing and entertaining. Their independence and cuddly ways always keep me guessing what they will do next. Likewise, box turtles and other "uncuddlies" are extremely interesting to observe. They are very different from other quadrupeds. A house is not a home without pets!

Figure 20. Example of a complete essay draft.

5. Students save the document as "essay title.draft" in the proper folder or directory.

6. Students print the document in color or print it and highlight it by hand.

7. Students give the draft to a proofreader for review.

Example Essay Draft

Figure 20 is a beginning essay (based on the basic paragraph "My Pets" from Structured Writing) written by a class of fifth graders with dyslexia after a year and a half of experience with the Structured Writing process. They learned to compose the various expository paragraphs in Structured Writing, and after practicing introductory and concluding paragraphs, they used information about family pets to stretch a basic paragraph into a five-paragraph essay.

The Publishing Step

When students receive approved essay drafts, the writing process is complete except for removing the color code and printing a final copy.

1. Students consider the proofreader's suggestions and make the necessary corrections. When any changes are made, students are asked to reread and check spelling before resubmitting to a proofreader.

2. Students then change the text color to black.

3. They save the document in the appropriate folder or directory as "essay title.final copy."

4. Students print a final copy in black.

5. Students submit to the teacher a complete packet containing the outline, organizer, draft, and final copy.

Summary

In summary, the Paragraph to Essay Lesson encompasses all previously taught Structured Writing lessons. Individual paragraphs are combined into one complex document, including:

◆ An **introductory paragraph**

◆ Three **supporting paragraphs** with **transition sentences**

◆ A **concluding paragraph**

Students comfortable with the Structured Writing process are usually delighted and relieved to see how it can be applied to writing essays and reports. Most students are capable of writing one paragraph at a time within an essay. The progression provides distinct places for students to take breaks that can also be used as mini-goals during the process of writing an essay or report. It is necessary to reinforce the process if students try to take shortcuts.

The writing process is the same throughout this program. Students follow the same process for each type of paragraph within an essay. The planning and outlining steps use Inspiration with teacher-created webs. The writing step uses a word processing program and teacher-created organizers. The editing step follows the same sequence for all writing. The process culminates with the formatting and publishing steps. Although the types of essays and multiple paragraph reports vary, the process and sequence remain the same.

In the Structured Writing II process, teachers emphasize content and complexity while the built-in structure of the process reinforces the essential elements of the specific essays being composed. Students must practice writing all kinds of essays. This can be accomplished in many ways. I have students outline many essays before deciding which ones they will write. Using the same topic, but dissimilar purposes, students can experiment using the various types of introductory and concluding techniques. Also, organizing ideas using different paragraph types allows students to write for specific purposes. It is essential for teachers to model ways to determine which types of paragraphs to use and how and when to use them. Writing shorter essays to begin with allows for more practice. By gradually adding length and complexity, students learn to consider the types of paragraphs that will best explain an idea or concept within an essay.

For practice, model lessons requiring three specific paragraph types to make up the body of an essay. For example, assign pupils to write a basic paragraph about the essential character-istics of a successful student. From this paragraph, assign a five-paragraph essay that must include a reason paragraph, an example paragraph, and a process paragraph. Students must decide which quality or student behavior can best be explained by the different para-graph types required by the assignment. They choose the introductory and concluding methods individually. This activity emphasizes paragraph and essay structure, but it also allows room for students to begin developing their individual voices. As students become more confident with essay structure, their writing becomes more original and self-assured.

Evaluation Rubric

Teachers should use the Paragraph to Essay Rubric to establish the writing level of students and evaluate their progress. It focuses on student aptitude in filling out the essay template and evaluates their writing mechanics. It highlights the editing process, spotlighting appropriate use of the spelling checker and text-to-speech features to further support independence and promote accuracy.

Paragraph to Essay Rubric

STRUCTURE	EMERGING	DEVELOPING	PROFICIENT
Introduction	Introductory paragraph contains: ◆ Thesis/focus sentence	Introductory paragraph contains: ◆ Thesis/focus sentence ◆ Plan/sequence of support topics	Introductory paragraph contains: ◆ Thesis/focus sentence ◆ Plan/sequence of support topics ◆ Introductory comments ◆ Attention-getter
Body	Body contains at least three supporting paragraphs that: ◆ Relate to the thesis/focus sentence	Body contains at least three supporting paragraphs that: ◆ Develop the thesis/focus sentence ◆ Are presented in logical order	Body contains at least three supporting paragraphs that: ◆ Develop the thesis/focus sentence ◆ Are presented in logical order ◆ Use transition sentences to link paragraphs
Conclusion	Concluding paragraph contains: ◆ Reference to thesis/focus sentence	Concluding paragraph contains: ◆ Reference to thesis/focus sentence ◆ Summary of body paragraphs	Concluding paragraph contains: ◆ Reference to thesis/focus sentence ◆ Summary of body paragraphs ◆ Effective use of closing techniques/clincher

MECHANICS	EMERGING	DEVELOPING	PROFICIENT
Capitalization	Correct capitalization of: ◆ Sentences	Correct capitalization of: ◆ Sentences ◆ Proper nouns	Correct capitalization of: ◆ Sentences ◆ Proper nouns ◆ Titles ◆ Quotations
Punctuation	Correct use of: ◆ Sentence-ending punctuation	Correct use of: ◆ Sentence-ending punctuation ◆ Quotation marks	Correct use of: ◆ Sentence-ending punctuation ◆ Quotation marks ◆ Commas ◆ Apostrophes
Spelling	Spelling is: ◆ Correct enough to read ◆ Inconsistently checked with spelling checker	Spelling is: ◆ Correct ◆ Effectively checked with spelling checker ◆ Checked with text-to-speech feature	Spelling is: ◆ Correct ◆ Effectively checked with spelling checker ◆ Checked with text-to-speech feature ◆ Correct for homonyms and proper nouns

Suggested Topics for Paragraph to Essay

Begin with a basic paragraph from Structured Writing or write a basic paragraph and then "stretch" it into a five-paragraph essay.

- ▸ My Pets
- ▸ Television Shows
- ▸ Video Games
- ▸ School Sports
- ▸ Successful Students
- ▸ Ways I Am Smart
- ▸ Too Much Homework
- ▸ Vacations
- ▸ Holidays

Successful Students

- ◆ Examples of success
- ◆ Reasons why success is important
- ◆ Process (ways) to become a successful student

Ways I Am Smart (Multiple Intelligences)

- ◆ Examples
- ◆ Classifications of intelligence
- ◆ Compare and contrast learning strengths and difficulties

Five-Paragraph Essay Planner

I. Introductory Paragraph
Attention-getter
Introductory comments
Thesis/focus sentence
Plan/sequence of three main ideas

II. First Supporting Paragraph
Topic sentence (refer to the first main idea)
First supporting sentence and details, ideas, quotes, elaboration
Second supporting sentence and details, ideas, quotes, elaboration
Third supporting sentence and details, ideas, quotes, elaboration
Concluding sentence (for this paragraph)

III. Second Supporting Paragraph
Topic sentence/transition sentence (connect to second main idea)
First supporting sentence and details, ideas, quotes, elaboration
Second supporting sentence and details, ideas, quotes, elaboration
Third supporting sentence and details, ideas, quotes, elaboration
Concluding sentence (for this paragraph)

IV. Third Supporting Paragraph
Topic sentence/transition sentence (connect to third main idea)
First supporting sentence and details, ideas, quotes, elaboration
Second supporting sentence and details, ideas, quotes, elaboration
Third supporting sentence and details, ideas, quotes, elaboration
Concluding sentence (for this paragraph)

V. Concluding Paragraph
Restate thesis/focus sentence (paraphrase)
Review three main ideas (keep it short) and details, ideas, quotes
Clincher sentence

Chapter 5

Expository Essays

Once students have mastered writing the various paragraphs using the Structured Writing process, practiced writing introductory and concluding paragraphs using the Structured Writing II method, and expanded paragraphs into essays, they are ready to compose specific expository essays. Instructors may follow the same sequence for teaching expository paragraph writing to teach expository essay composition (reason, example, process, classification, and compare and contrast). Student expository paragraphs can be expanded into expository essays using the same process described in the previous chapter.

The expository essay is the academic writing assignment most often required of students, one that requires them to gather, organize, and present their thoughts about a course-related topic. Its purpose is to present information in a way that demonstrates a clear understanding of the subject. It speaks with conviction, flows logically, and uses correct grammar, capitalization, and punctuation. The specific purpose will vary with the assignment; it may be to explain something using reasons or examples; to identify the steps in a process; to classify, compare, or contrast; to assess cause and effect; or to argue for or against a policy or opinion.

The expository essay uses a long-established five-paragraph essay form starting with an introductory paragraph with a thesis/focus sentence, three supporting paragraphs (the body), and a concluding paragraph. Students organize their writing with the thesis/focus sentence and follow it with reasons, examples, and details to support it. Expository essays are intended for an audience of teachers and fellow students, are written in a moderately formal voice, and typically use a third-person point of view. If the writing focuses on personal experience, a first-person point of view is appropriate. Words are prudently chosen to plainly state one's understanding of a topic.

Expository essays in Structured Writing II are separated into five different types according to their purpose: reason, example, process, classification, and compare and contrast.

- **Reason essay:** employs reason paragraphs to explain an event, perspective, or incident

- **Example essay:** uses example paragraphs to make something easier to understand

- **Process essay:** uses process paragraphs to explain a procedure

- **Classification essay:** uses classification paragraphs (categories, groups) to clarify the location of something within a larger schema or framework

- **Compare and contrast essay:** uses paragraphs that compare and contrast to explain how an event or idea is like or not like a comparable event or idea

The goal for students is to learn to incorporate various paragraph types within an essay to demonstrate their understanding of a subject. Students with experience using the Structured Writing process and Inspiration have learned to manipulate the various paragraph webs and outlines to customize templates for specific assignments. For instance, a student assigned to write an essay about his or her learning strengths (multiple intelligences) might use an example paragraph to illustrate ways he or she is smart, a classification paragraph to categorize and explain the theory of multiple intelligences, and a compare and contrast paragraph to examine his or her relative strengths and weaknesses.

Objectives

1. Students will write a specific type of expository essay using an introductory paragraph, three supporting paragraphs, and a concluding paragraph.

2. Students will use the steps of the Structured Writing II process to plan, write, edit, format, and publish a specific type of expository essay.

3. Students will use the sequential editing steps in the Structured Writing process. They will use text-to-speech features to read and listen while checking the writing content, capitalization, punctuation, word usage, and spelling. They will make revisions to increase sentence complexity and use a thesaurus to enhance vocabulary and eliminate overused words.

Materials Needed

Structured Writing II CD-ROM

◆ Expository Essay Webs

◆ Expository Essay Organizers

Inspiration 6.0 or 7.0

Word processing program

Posters

◆ Reason Essay Web

◆ Suggested Topics for Expository Essays

◆ Editing Steps (chapter 1)

◆ Possible Conclusions (chapter 3)

◆ Five-Paragraph Essay Planner (chapter 4)

Essential Elements

The Structured Writing II process teaches students to write an expository essay using:

1. An **introductory paragraph**

2. **Three supporting paragraphs** with **transition sentences**

3. A **concluding paragraph**

Color Codes

◆ White for the essay title

◆ Blue for paragraph types

◆ Yellow for topic and concluding sentences

◆ Green for supporting sentences

◆ Pink for details and elaboration

The Structured Writing II Process

Planning step: Outline the essay.

Writing step: Expand ideas into sentences. Organize sentences into paragraphs.

Editing step: Edit and revise one paragraph at a time.

Formatting step: Create a draft in essay format.

Publishing step: Print the final copy.

The Editing Process

1. Open the organizer file.

2. Use text-to-speech to read and listen to each sentence, one at a time, to check content. Edit and revise.

3. Check capitalization.

4. Check punctuation.

5. Check for homonyms and misused words.

6. Run a spelling checker.

7. Read and listen to changes using text-to-speech.

8. Save changes.

9. Print in color or print and highlight by hand.

10. Submit to a proofreader for review.

11. Make any necessary changes suggested by the proofreader.

12. Give to the teacher for feedback and approval.

The Expository Essay Process

The Planning Step

Students begin the planning step by opening the correct Inspiration template for the specific type of expository essay they are going to write (Reason Essay Web, Example Essay Web, Process Essay Web, Classification Essay Web, or Compare and Contrast Essay Web). These templates are on the CD-ROM accompanying this book. The Reason Essay Web, along with an example of the web filled out, are reproduced in poster form on the fold-out page in this chapter.

The templates help students plan the essay using reasons, examples, steps in a process, classifications, or similarities and differences between two entities. The color code and text identify the essential parts of the essay (title, introductory paragraph, three supporting paragraphs, and concluding paragraph) and the essential elements of each paragraph (topic sentence, supporting sentences, and concluding sentence). This chapter focuses on one example, the reason essay. Instructors can use any of the expository essay webs to create the other types of essays using the same process.

This lesson can use any expository paragraph and expand it into an essay. The essay could also be written as a response to a question that requires a specific type of answer, supported with a reason, examples, and so forth. For the latter, students must brainstorm using Rapid-Fire in Inspiration to generate ideas and a word bank.

RapidFire is an Inspiration feature that allows quick recording of ideas while brainstorming a topic. Students open a new Inspiration document in the diagram form and type in the word to brainstorm. Students click on RapidFire and a red lightning bolt icon appears in the box after the main idea. Students type in their ideas and click on Return after each new idea to record them in a web (Figure 21). Once ideas have been generated, students categorize them and then prioritize them for writing. This is an efficient way for students to determine writing topics and subtopics (Figures 22 and 23).

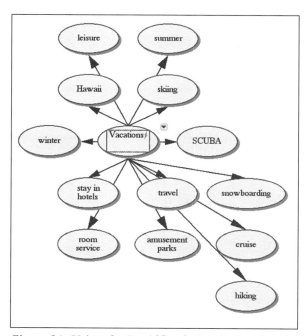

Figure 21. Using the Rapidfire feature in Inspiration enables quick brainstorming. In this example, the topic is vacations.

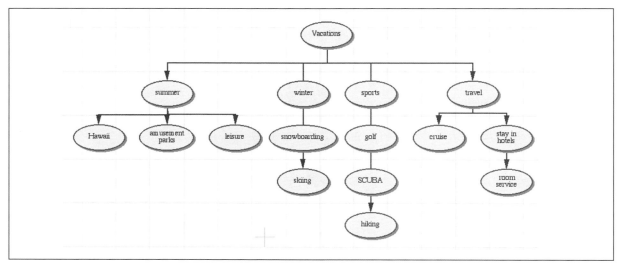

Figure 22. Vacation ideas categorized in web form.

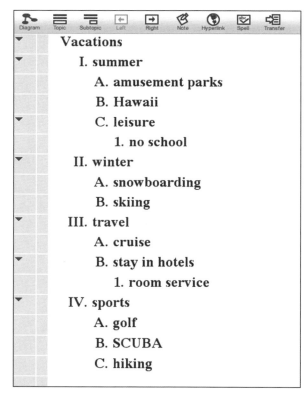

Figure 23. Vacation ideas categorized in outline form.

The topic I use in this chapter, vacations, can be modified to teach any of the expository essays. A variety of vacations could be described and explained in an example essay, for instance, or the steps needed to plan one could be detailed in a process essay. Vacations could be grouped by seasons, by activities, or by cost to compose a classification essay. Finally, students could compare the best and the worst vacations, or the most expensive and least expensive vacations, in a compare and contrast essay. (Refer to the poster Suggested Topics for Expository Essays for other themes.)

For the purpose of this lesson, the Reason Paragraph "Why I Like Vacations" from the first *Structured Writing* book will be used as a model (Figure 24). When modeling this lesson, be sure to show students how this individual paragraph can be expanded into a five-paragraph reason essay. Then assign students to create their own content using the Reason Essay Web. The Five-Paragraph Essay Planner poster in chapter 4 provides an outline for guidance through the planning process.

The topic sentence of the paragraph becomes the focus sentence in the introductory paragraph, the three supporting sentences are each expanded into separate reason paragraphs that

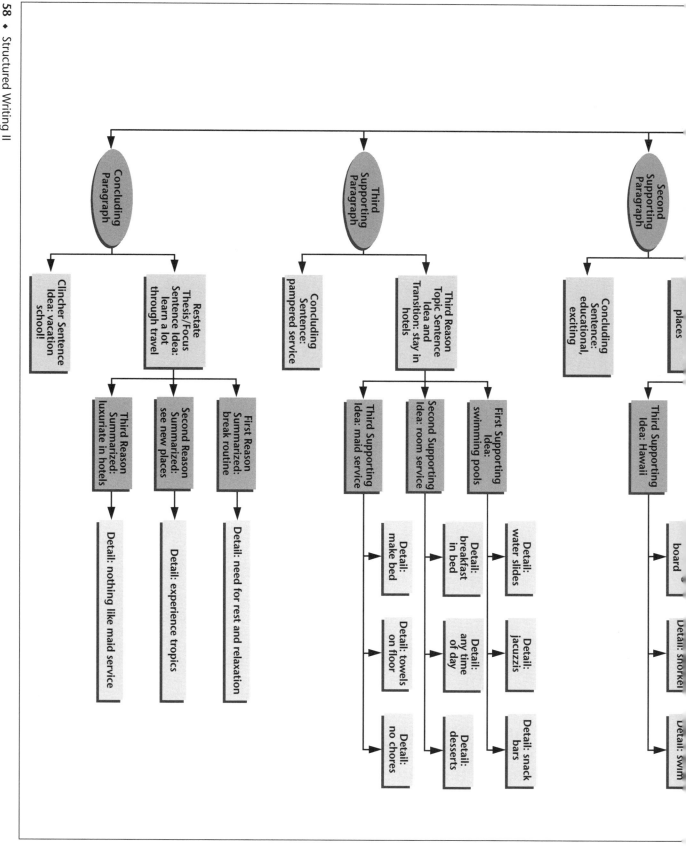

Concluding Paragraph

Clincher Sentence Idea: vacation school!

Restate Thesis/Focus Sentence Idea: learn a lot through travel

Third Reason Summarized: luxuriate in hotels → Detail: nothing like maid service

Second Reason Summarized: see new places → Detail: experience tropics

First Reason Summarized: break routine → Detail: need for rest and relaxation

Third Supporting Paragraph

Concluding Sentence: pampered service

Third Reason Topic Sentence Idea and Transition: stay in hotels

Third Supporting Idea: maid service → Detail: make bed / Detail: towels on floor / Detail: no chores

Second Supporting Idea: room service → Detail: breakfast in bed / Detail: any time of day / Detail: desserts

First Supporting Idea: swimming pools → Detail: water slides / Detail: jacuzzis / Detail: snack bars

Second Supporting Paragraph

Concluding Sentence: educational, exciting

places

Third Supporting Idea: Hawaii

board

Detail: snorkel

Detail: swim

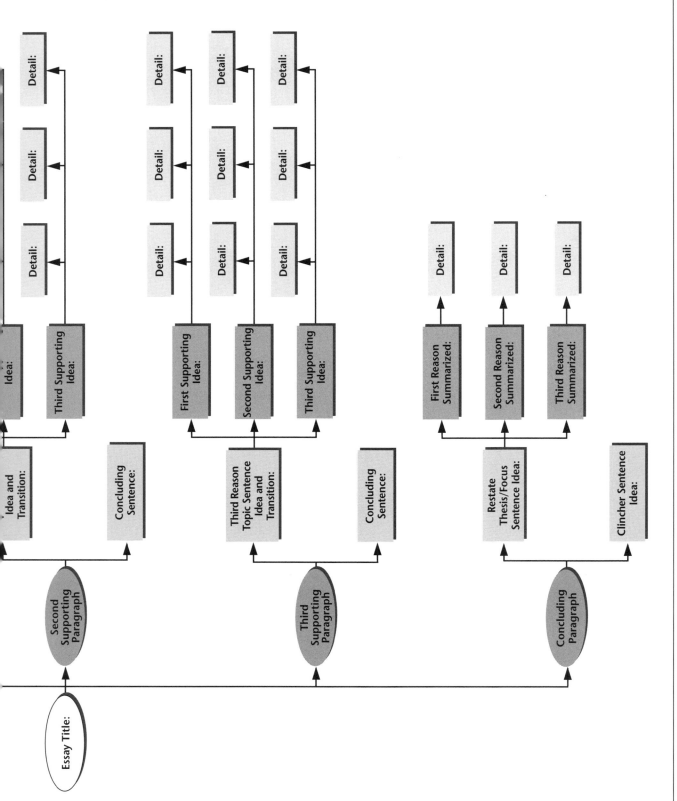

Reason Essay Web

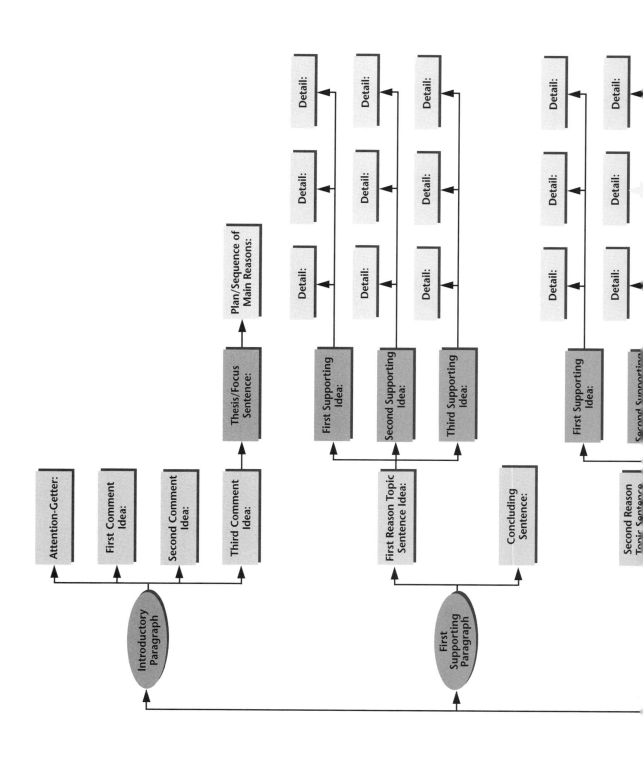

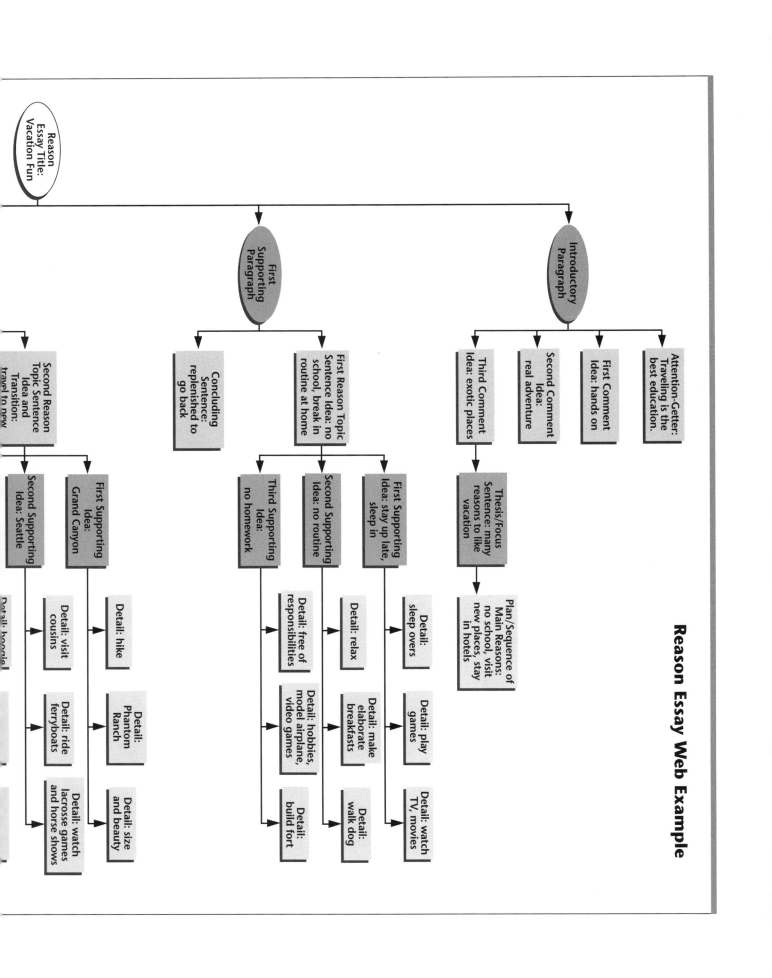

Reason Essay Web Example

Reason Essay Title: Vacation Fun

Introductory Paragraph
- Attention-Getter: Traveling is the best education.
- First Comment Idea: hands on
- Second Comment Idea: real adventure
- Third Comment Idea: exotic places
- Thesis/Focus Sentence: many reasons to like vacation
  - Plan/Sequence of Main Reasons: no school, visit new places, stay in hotels

First Supporting Paragraph
- Concluding Sentence: replenished to go back
- First Reason Topic Sentence Idea: no school, break in routine at home
  - First Supporting Idea: stay up late, sleep in
    - Detail: sleep overs
    - Detail: play games
    - Detail: watch TV, movies
  - Second Supporting Idea: no routine
    - Detail: relax
    - Detail: make elaborate breakfasts
    - Detail: walk dog
  - Third Supporting Idea: no homework
    - Detail: free of responsibilities
    - Detail: hobbies, model airplane, video games
    - Detail: build fort

Second Reason Topic Sentence Idea and Transition: travel to new
- First Supporting Idea: Grand Canyon
  - Detail: hike
  - Detail: Phantom Ranch
  - Detail: size and beauty
- Second Supporting Idea: Seattle
  - Detail: visit cousins
  - Detail: ride ferryboats
  - Detail: watch lacrosse games and horse shows

Student Name

Date

Why I Like Vacations

There are many reasons why I like to go on vacation. First of all, I like to go on vacation because I don't have to go to school. I can stay up later at night because I don't have to wake up early for school. I can sleep in later in the morning because I don't have to get up and go to school. A second reason I like to take vacations is because I like to visit new places. I want to see the Grand Canyon. I want to go and see my cousin in Seattle and ride the ferryboats. The third reason I like to go on vacation is because I like to stay in hotels. I like to swim in hotel swimming pools. I really like to order room service, especially for breakfast. These are just three reasons why I like to go on vacation.

Figure 24. A reason paragraph draft.

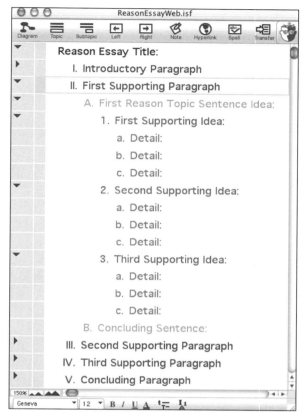

Figure 25. The Reason Essay Outline with only the first supporting paragraph showing.

make up the body of the essay, and the concluding sentence is expanded into a full, concluding paragraph. The following steps provide directions to completing the planning step.

1. Students open the Reason Essay Web. The white box indicates the place for the essay title, and the blue ovals identify the paragraph types, or functions, within the essay. The yellow boxes are for topic and concluding sentence ideas within each paragraph, and the green boxes signify the places for supporting sentence ideas. The pink boxes are for the details about the supporting ideas.

2. With the exception of the thesis/focus sentence, students type key words and short phrases into the Reason Essay Web to represent their ideas. (The foldout page in this chapter shows the Reason Essay Web on one side and the Reason Essay Web

with the pet ideas filled in on the other side.) **Reinforce the distinction between organizing ideas by outlining and actually writing sentences.** It is important that students organize their ideas for the essay as a whole before starting to write. The body paragraphs will differ in type and order depending on the purpose of the essay. It is best to make this determination in the planning step. The words and phrases will then be converted into an outline to use as a guide for writing each paragraph later in the writing step.

3. When all the boxes are completed, students convert the web into a color-coded outline by selecting the Outline option in Inspiration. If changes need to be made in the order of the paragraphs, it is easier to rearrange them in the outline format. Students run the spelling checker and save

Reason Essay Outline

Reason Essay Title:

I. **Introductory Paragraph**
    A. Attention-Getter:
    B. First Comment Idea:
    C. Second Comment Idea:
    D. Third Comment Idea:
       1. Thesis/Focus Sentence:
          a. Plan/Sequence of Main Reasons:

II. **First Supporting Paragraph**
    A. First Reason Topic Sentence Idea:
       1. First Supporting Idea:
          a. Detail:
          b. Detail:
          c. Detail:
       2. Second Supporting Idea:
          a. Detail:
          b. Detail:
          c. Detail:
       3. Third Supporting Idea:
          a. Detail:
          b. Detail:
          c. Detail:
    B. Concluding Sentence:

III. **Second Supporting Paragraph**
    A. Second Reason Topic Sentence Idea and Transition:
       1. First Supporting Idea:
          a. Detail:
          b. Detail:
          c. Detail:

       2. Second Supporting Idea:
          a. Detail:
          b. Detail:
          c. Detail:
       3. Third Supporting Idea:
          a. Detail:
          b. Detail:
          c. Detail:
    B. Concluding Sentence:

IV. **Third Supporting Paragraph**
    A. Third Reason Topic Sentence Idea and Transition:
       1. First Supporting Idea:
          a. Detail:
          b. Detail:
          c. Detail:
       2. Second Supporting Idea:
          a. Detail:
          b. Detail:
          c. Detail:
       3. Third Supporting Idea:
          a. Detail:
          b. Detail:
          c. Detail:
    B. Concluding Sentence:

V. **Concluding Paragraph**
    A. Restate Thesis/Focus Sentence Idea:
       1. First Reason Summarized:
          a. Detail:
       2. Second Reason Summarized:
          a. Detail:
       3. Third Reason Summarized:
          a. Detail:
    B. Clincher Sentence Idea:

Figure 26. The complete Reason Essay Outline template.

the Reason Essay Outline as "essay title.outline" in the appropriate folder or directory. Figure 26 shows the Reason Essay Outline template and Figure 27 shows the Reason Essay Outline with the vacation ideas filled in.

4. Some students may be overwhelmed or distracted by the entire essay while working on individual paragraphs. To simplify the visuals, simply choose Hide Subtopics in the Inspiration outline format and let students view only one paragraph at a time while they write. Figure 25 shows an outline with just the First Supporting Paragraph displayed in full detail.

5. When students are ready to print their outlines, they must first go to View in the main menu, then to Notes, and check Hide All to hide the notes on the outline. Then, students go to File in the main menu, scroll to Page Setup, and uncheck Hidden Notes (see chapter 3 for more information). These steps will keep the notes from appearing on the printed document.

Example Reason Essay Outline

Reason Essay Title: Vacation Fun

I. Introductory Paragraph

   A. Attention-Getter: Traveling is the best education.

   B. First Comment Idea: hands-on

   C. Second Comment Idea: real adventure

   D. Third Comment Idea: exotic places

     1. Thesis/Focus Sentence: many reasons to like vacation

       a. Plan/Sequence of Main Reasons: no school, visit new places, stay in hotels

II. First Supporting Paragraph

   A. First Reason Topic Sentence Idea: no school, break in routine at home

     1. First Supporting Idea: stay up late, sleep in

       a. Detail: sleep overs

       b. Detail: play games

       c. Detail: watch TV, movies

     2. Second Supporting Idea: no routine

       a. Detail: relax

       b. Detail: make elaborate breakfasts

       c. Detail: walk dog

     3. Third Supporting Idea: no homework

       a. Detail: free of responsibilities

       b. Detail: hobbies, model airplanes, video games

       c. Detail: build fort

   B. Concluding Sentence: replenished to go back

III. Second Supporting Paragraph

   A. Second Reason Topic Sentence Idea and Transition: travel to new places

     1. First Supporting Idea: Grand Canyon

       a. Detail: hike

       b. Detail: Phantom Ranch

       c. Detail: size and beauty

     2. Second Supporting Idea: Seattle

       a. Detail: visit cousins

       b. Detail: ride ferryboats

       c. Detail: watch horse shows

     3. Third Supporting Idea: Hawaii

       a. Detail: boogie board

       b. Detail: snorkel

       c. Detail: swim

   B. Concluding Sentence: educational, exciting

IV. Third Supporting Paragraph

   A. Third Reason Topic Sentence Idea and Transition: stay in hotels

     1. First Supporting Idea: swimming pools

       a. Detail: water slides

       b. Detail: jacuzzis

       c. Detail: snack bars

     2. Second Supporting Idea: room service

       a. Detail: breakfast in bed

       b. Detail: any time of day

       c. Detail: desserts

     3. Third Supporting Idea: maid service

       a. Detail: make bed

       b. Detail: towels on floor

       c. Detail: no chores

   B. Concluding Sentence: pampered service

V. Concluding Paragraph

   A. Restate Thesis/Focus Sentence Idea: learn a lot through travel

     1. First Reason Summarized: break routine

       a. Detail: need for rest and relaxation

     2. Second Reason Summarized: see new places

       a. Detail: experience tropics

     3. Third Reason Summarized: luxuriate in hotels

       a. Detail: nothing like maid service

   B. Clincher Sentence Idea: vacation school!

Figure 27. A Reason Essay Outline filled in with a student's ideas about vacations.

6. Students print the color-coded outline or print it and highlight it by hand.

7. Students give the outline to the teacher for review.

The teacher checks for content, order, and completeness to give feedback to the students before they begin the writing step. Reassured that they are on the right track, students use the outline to guide their efforts when writing.

The Writing Step

Students open the Reason Essay Organizer in the coordinating word processing program to begin the writing step (Figure 28). They expand the ideas from their outlines into complete sentences in the organizer, one sentence at a time, one paragraph at a time.

Again, the amount of instructional time available per class will determine the number of writing steps that can be covered in a lesson. Essays are more easily written one paragraph at a time after the whole process has been explained and modeled. Particular students may need extra time to complete assignments; for those students who have difficulty staying

---

Reason Essay Organizer

    Reason Essay Organizer by:
    Essay Title:

Introductory Paragraph
    Attention-Getter:
    First Comment:
    Second Comment:
    Third Comment:
    Thesis/Focus Sentence:
    Plan/Sequence of Main Reasons:

First Supporting Paragraph
    First Reason Topic Sentence:
    First Supporting Reason:
    Detail:
    Detail:
    Detail:
    Second Supporting Reason:
    Detail:
    Detail:
    Detail:
    Third Supporting Reason:
    Detail:
    Detail:
    Detail:
    Concluding Sentence:

Second Supporting Paragraph
    Second Reason Topic Sentence and Transition:
    First Supporting Reason:
    Detail:
    Detail:
    Detail:

    Second Supporting Reason:
    Detail:
    Detail:
    Detail:
    Third Supporting Reason:
    Detail:
    Detail:
    Detail:
    Concluding Sentence:

Third Supporting Paragraph
    Third Reason Topic Sentence and Transition:
    First Supporting Reason:
    Detail:
    Detail:
    Detail:
    Second Supporting Reason:
    Detail:
    Detail:
    Detail:
    Third Supporting Reason:
    Detail:
    Detail:
    Detail:
    Concluding Sentence:

Concluding Paragraph
    Restate Thesis/Focus Sentence:
    First Reason Summarized:
    Detail:
    Second Reason Summarized:
    Detail:
    Third Reason Summarized:
    Detail:
    Clincher Sentence:

Figure 28. The complete Reason Essay Organizer template.

on-task, the completion of individual steps in the process can serve as mini-goals and natural rest breaks, increasing their sense of accomplishment. Customize the process to fit instructional time constraints and to accommodate student needs.

Compose the Introductory Paragraph

Students begin the writing step by composing a forthright and precise thesis/focus sentence that **clearly states the main idea of the essay.** The main purpose of the essay is identified to determine the direction for the writing and provide the order of the supporting paragraphs. After the body of the essay has been composed, students try various introduction techniques to get the reader's attention and open the essay. They develop the gateway using related comments and details to "hook" the reader. The introductory paragraph's plan/sequence of main points reveals the order of the supporting paragraphs to follow.

Teachers remind students of the essential elements of the introductory paragraph:

- An **attention-getter**
- **Introductory comments**
- A **thesis/focus sentence**
- A **plan (sequence) of support paragraphs**

Following the Structured Writing II process, students use the introductory paragraph section in the Reason Essay Organizer to expand their ideas for the outline into complete sentences (Figure 29). Text cues indicate the appropriate information, and the color code reinforces the paragraph structure. Teachers direct students to take into account the purpose of their essays and the tone of the opening, choosing colorful adjectives and strong verbs to "hook" the reader (see chapter 2, the Introductory Paragraph Lesson). When the introductory paragraph sentences are complete, the students save them as "essay title.organizer" in the proper folder or directory.

Example Reason Essay Organizer— Introductory Paragraph

> **Reason Essay by:** Student Name
> **Essay Title:** Vacations
> **Introductory Paragraph**
> **Attention-Getter:**
> **First Comment:**
> **Second Comment:**
> **Third Comment:**
> **Thesis/Focus Sentence:** There are many reasons why I like to go on vacations.
> **Plan/Sequence of Main Reasons:** I don't have to go to school, I visit new places, and I stay in fancy hotels.

Figure 29. A partially filled in organizer.

Compose the Supporting Paragraphs

Students use the color-coded Reason Essay Organizer template and a word processing program to guide and expand their ideas from the outline into complete sentences in the supporting paragraph sections of the organizer, one paragraph at a time.

1. Students begin by writing the topic sentence for the first body paragraph. They use the first supporting sentence from the basic paragraph "Why I Like Vacations" as the topic sentence for the first supporting paragraph in the essay. The supporting sentence in the reason paragraph, "First of all, I like to go on vacation because I don't have to go to school," is expanded to "I especially like to go on vacation because I don't have to go to school," the topic sentence for the first body paragraph in this essay. Writers follow their outlines to compose the first supporting paragraph, elaborating and writing supporting detail sentences, one at a time. They make sure sentences are complete and clearly express their thoughts. Each paragraph will be edited and revised in the editing step.

2. Point out to students that the second supporting sentence from the basic paragraph, "The second reason I like to take

Example Reason Essay Organizer—Supporting Paragraphs

Reason Essay Organizer by: Student Name
Essay Title: Vacations

Introductory Paragraph

First Supporting Paragraph

First Reason Topic Sentence: I especially like to go on vacation because I don't have to go to school.

First Supporting Reason: I can stay up late at night, and I don't have to get up early the next morning.

Detail: My friends and I have sleepovers.

Detail: We can play games into the night.

Detail: We can watch videos or TV later than usual.

Second Supporting Reason: *Also*, there is no routine at home during vacation.

Detail: Everyone can relax any way she or he chooses.

Detail: I like to make elaborate breakfasts when I finally get out of bed.

Detail: I can walk the dog whenever he wants to go.

Third Supporting Reason: *Most important*, I have no homework!

Detail: I'm free of school responsibilities.

Detail: I can make model airplanes and do my other hobbies instead of study.

Detail: I can play outside and build my tree fort.

Concluding Sentence: A break from school helps me energize to go back.

Second Supporting Paragraph

Second Reason Topic Sentence and Transition: I am free to travel to new places.

First Supporting Reason: *Once* I got to go to the Grand Canyon in Arizona.

Detail: I hiked the Bright Angel Trail with my scout troupe all the way to the bottom.

Detail: We stayed overnight at the Phantom Ranch.

Detail: We experienced the grandness and beauty of this national park.

Second Supporting Reason: I *also* like to travel to Seattle, Washington.

Detail: My cousins live on Vashon Island, and I like to visit them there.

Detail: We have to ride the ferryboats to get on and off the island because there are no bridges.

Detail: I sometimes watch my cousin play lacrosse and my aunt compete in Appaloosa horse shows.

Third Supporting Reason: *Next*, I'd like to fly to Hawaii with my family.

Detail: I would like to boogie board at the big wave beaches.

Detail: I dream about snorkeling at a coral reef among exotic tropical fish.

Detail: Swimming all day in warm water and sunshine sounds heavenly.

Concluding Sentence: Travel experience is educational, fun, and exciting.

Third Supporting Paragraph

Third Reason Topic Sentence and Transition: I love staying in fancy hotels.

First Supporting Reason: *First of all*, hotels usually have terrific swimming pools.

Detail: Many have water slides and sections to play water polo.

Detail: Hot tubs with Jacuzzi jets top off nighttime swimming.

Detail: Snack bars are located at hotel pools to satisfy hungry guests like me.

Second Supporting Reason: *Second*, room service is another good reason to vacation in a hotel.

Detail: I love to order breakfast in bed.

Detail: You can order just about any food any time of day with room service.

Detail: I especially like the way desserts are served in fancy glass dishes.

Third Supporting Reason: *Finally*, maid service means no chores for me!

Detail: I don't have to make my bed when I stay in a hotel.

Detail: I am supposed to throw my wet towels on the bathroom floor so the maid will know to change them.

Detail: I feel like a king with maid service.

Concluding Sentence: Recreation and being pampered make staying in elegant hotels fantastic.

Figure 30. Transition words are underlined and italicized.

vacations is because I like to visit new places," is expanded into the topic sentence for the second body paragraph, "Since I don't have to go to school, I am free to travel to new places." Students follow the model and elaborate their sentences in the writing step.

3. Encourage students to use adjective and adverb modifiers and prepositional phrases to clarify their prose.

4. Prompt students to combine simple sentences into compound sentences, to use complex sentences, and to vary sentence structure.

5. Encourage students to consult a thesaurus to eliminate overused words, improve vocabulary, and enhance the intricacy of their written expression.

6. Remind students to use appropriate transition words in the green structure sentences to indicate the main points within each paragraph.

Once the sentences in the first supporting paragraph are completed, the students add it to the organizer by saving it as "essay title.organizer" in the proper folder or directory. They then move on to the second supporting paragraph, compose the sentences, and add the second paragrapn to the organizer by saving it once again as "essay title.organizer." They follow the same process for the third supporting paragraph in the body of the essay. Transition words appear in italic and are underlined (Figure 30).

Transitions

While modeling the body paragraphs of the expository essay with students, review and highlight the use of **transition words** to connect ideas and **transition sentences** to connect paragraphs. Transition sentences link the body paragraphs within the essay, connecting the ideas in one paragraph with those in the following paragraph to maintain a smooth flow of ideas. The Structured Writing II process teaches the use of transition words and phrases in the topic sentences of the second and third body paragraphs. Generating examples of transition sentences helps students to use them with confidence. Figure 31 shows the transitions in italic and underlined.

Compose the Concluding Paragraph

Adhering to the Structured Writing process, students use the concluding paragraph section in the Reason Essay Organizer to expand their closing ideas into sentences, one at a time (Figure 32). Text cues indicate the required information, and the color code reinforces the paragraph structure. Encourage students to take a stand when deciding how to end their essays. Remind students to consider the audience and purpose for writing the essay, the tone they have established, and the points made to create a memorable conclusion. They can answer any questions unanswered in the body paragraphs, summarize the main points, or emphasize the special importance of one of the main points. Conclusion paragraphs restate the focus or primary message, and say something that will

---

Example Transition Sentences for Second and Third Supporting Paragraphs

Reason Essay Organizer by: Student Name

First Supporting Paragraph

First Reason Topic Sentence: I especially like to go on vacation because I don't have to go to school.

Second Supporting Paragraph

Second Reason Topic Sentence and Transition: *Since I don't have to go to school*, I am free to travel to new places.

Third Supporting Paragraph

Third Reason Topic Sentence and Transition: *In addition to leisure time and travel*, I love staying in fancy hotels.

Figure 31. Transition words are underlined and italicized.

keep the readers thinking about the subject. Leaving readers with a strong image, or perhaps a bit of wit, effectively "wraps up" a composition (see the Possible Conclusions poster at the end of chapter 3). When teaching this section, emphasize the essential elements of the essay's concluding paragraph:

- A **topic sentence restating or echoing the thesis/focus sentence** (from the introductory paragraph)

- **Three supporting sentences** referring to each of the main points

- **Details** for each of the supporting sentences

- A **clincher sentence**

When the concluding paragraph sentences are complete, the students add it to the organizer by saving it as "essay title.organizer" in the proper folder or directory.

Frequently, writing the concluding paragraph first is appropriate, especially when students are writing persuasive essays. Students can initially write a conclusion paragraph outline and then prepare the various body paragraph outlines to either deductively, inductively, or chronologically establish their perspective. Alerting students to the options they will need to consider when planning an essay is crucial and efficiently taught by modeling.

The Editing Step

Students edit one paragraph at a time within the Reason Essay Organizer using the Structured Writing process. Students check capitalization, punctuation, homonyms, and spelling in the specific order described in the Structured Writing editing process. Encourage students to consult the Editing Steps poster (chapter 1) to remind them of the editing procedures.

1. Students open their saved organizer, "essay title.organizer."

2. Students read and listen to each paragraph, one sentence at a time, using the text-to-speech features to check the content of their writing. Each separate paragraph is edited as a whole within the entire multi-paragraph essay.

   - Students add, delete, rearrange, and change words until the sentences sound "right" and communicate their intended meaning. The students practice varying the sentence structure, using different kinds of sentences, and consulting a thesaurus to increase the complexity of the vocabulary.

   - They specifically check for appropriate transition sentences between the second and third body paragraphs.

3. Students check capitalization.

Example Reason Essay Organizer—Concluding Paragraph

Reason Essay Organizer by: Student Name

Concluding Paragraph

Restate Thesis/Focus Sentence: There are so many good reasons to take a vacation.

First Reason Summarized: Spontaneity could replace school time routines.

Detail: Rest and relaxation would be part of the "Three Rs."

Second Reason Summarized: Traveling places would replace just reading about them in textbooks.

Detail: I'd really look forward to studying a unit on Hawaii!

Third Reason Summarized: Hotel living with room service would top off the whole experience.

Detail: Maybe I could order a tutor to help with homework?

Clincher Sentence: I wish I could attend the School of Vacations!

Figure 32. The concluding paragraph of an essay organizer filled in.

4. Students check punctuation.

5. Students check word usage, including homonyms and misused words.

6. Students check spelling.

7. Students read and listen to changes using text-to-speech.

8. Students save their edited organizers as "essay title.organizer" in the appropriate folder or directory. This will replace the unedited organizer.

9. Students print the document in color or print it and highlight it by hand.

10. Students give the document to a proof-reader for review.

11. Students make any necessary changes suggested by the proofreader.

12. Students submit the document to the teacher for feedback and approval.

Teachers assess the sentences and paragraphs in the organizer for appropriate content, proper syntax, and sentence variation. Once edited organizers are approved, students move to the formatting step.

Students have now edited the individual paragraph organizers within the essay, one at a time. These paragraphs have been saved in the reason essay folder and are now ready to be formatted into the complete essay and saved as "essay title.draft."

The Formatting Step

In this step, students prepare the document for publishing. The structure words are deleted and the sentences are put in proper paragraph form as learned in the Structured Writing process, one paragraph at a time. The color code remains to reinforce paragraph structure within the essay.

1. Students put the required heading on the document, such as their name and the date.

2. Students highlight the structure cues and delete them. They maintain appropriate spacing after ending punctuation (one or two spaces) and between lines (single, one and a half, or double spacing). The same procedure is used for each of the remaining paragraphs.

3. The authors center the essay title and indent topic sentences.

4. Students read and listen to the entire essay, paying attention to the flow of ideas.

5. Students save the document as "essay title.draft" in the proper folder or directory.

6. Students print the document in color or print it and highlight it by hand.

7. Students give the draft to a proofreader for review.

The essay draft in Figure 33 is a compilation of the writing of three seventh graders with dyslexia. They had approximately a year and a half of experience using the Structured Writing process. Each had various reasons for enjoying vacations, but they all agreed on a few: no school, travel, and room service are among the best reasons to take vacations. They later used the same topic to write example, classification, and compare and contrast essays.

The Publishing Step

When students receive their approved essay drafts back from the proofreader, the writing process is complete except for removing the color code and printing a final copy.

1. Students consider the proofreader's suggestions and make the necessary corrections. When any changes are made, students are to reread and run another spelling check before resubmitting to a proofreader.

2. Students then change the text color to black.

Student Name

Date

Vacations

Traveling is the best education. When you travel, you can focus on leisure time. Adventure can also be part of the package. It's wonderful to visit exotic and historical places. There are many reasons why I like to go on vacation. I don't have to go to school, I visit new places, and I stay in fancy hotels.

I especially like vacation because I don't have to go to school. I can stay up late at night, and I don't have to get up early the next morning. My friends and I can sleep over at each other's house. We can play games into the night. We can watch videos or TV later than usual. Also, there is no routine at home during vacation. Everyone can relax any way she or he chooses. I like to make elaborate breakfasts when I finally get out of bed. I can walk the dog whenever he wants to go. Most important, I have no homework! I'm free of school responsibilities. I can make model airplanes and do my other hobbies instead of study. I can play outside and build my tree fort. A break from school helps me energize to go back.

Since I don't have to go to school, I am free to travel to new places. Once I got to go to the Grand Canyon in Arizona on vacation. I hiked the Bright Angel Trail with my scout troop all the way to the bottom. We stayed overnight at the Phantom Ranch. We experienced the grandness and beauty of this national park. Also, I took a trip to Seattle, Washington. My cousins live on Vashon Island, and I like to visit them there. We have to ride the ferryboats to get on and off the island because there are no bridges. I sometimes watch my cousin play lacrosse and my aunt compete in Appaloosa horse shows. Next, I'd like to fly to Hawaii with my family. I would like to boogie board at the big wave beaches. I have dreams of snorkeling above a coral reef among exotic tropical fish. Swimming all day in warm water and sunshine sounds heavenly. Traveling is educational, fun, and exciting.

In addition to leisure time and travel, I love staying in fancy hotels. First of all, hotels usually have terrific swimming pools. Many have water slides and sections to play water polo. Hot tubs with Jacuzzi jets top off nighttime swimming. Snack bars are located at hotel pools to satisfy hungry guests like me. Second, room service is another good reason to vacation in a hotel. I love to order breakfast in bed. You can order just about any food any time of day with room service. I especially like the way desserts are served in fancy glass dishes. Finally, maid service means no chores for me! I don't have to make my bed when I stay in a hotel. I am supposed to throw my wet towels on the bathroom floor so the maid will know to change them. I feel like a king with maid service. Recreation and being pampered make staying in elegant hotels fantastic.

There are so many good reasons to take a vacation. Spontaneity could replace school time routines. Rest and relaxation would be part of the "Three Rs." Traveling places would replace just reading about them in textbooks. I'd really look forward to studying a unit on Hawaii! Hotel living with room service would top off the whole experience. Maybe I could order a tutor to help with homework? I wish I could attend the School of Vacations!

Figure 33. An example of a completed reason essay draft.

3. They save the document in the appropriate folder or directory as "essay title.final copy."

4. Students print a final copy in black.

5. Students submit to the teacher a complete packet containing the outline, organizer, draft, and final copy.

Summary

In summary, the Expository Essay Lesson encompasses all previously taught Structured Writing lessons. Individual paragraphs are combined into one complex document, including:

◆ An **introductory paragraph**

◆ Three **supporting paragraphs** with **transition sentences**

◆ A **concluding paragraph**

Students experienced in the Structured Writing process are usually delighted and relieved to see how it can be applied to writing essays and reports. Most students are capable of writing one paragraph at a time within an essay. The progression provides distinct places for students to take breaks, and completing a paragraph can be pursued as a mini-goal. Reinforce the process if students try to take shortcuts.

Structured Writing II emphasizes content and complexity. The built-in structure of the Structured Writing process reinforces the essential elements of the specific essays being composed. Students must practice writing all kinds of essays. This can be accomplished in many ways. First, have students outline many essays before deciding which ones they will write. Using the same topic, but dissimilar purposes, students can experiment using the various types of introductory and concluding techniques. Organizing ideas using different paragraph types allows students to write for specific purposes. It is essential for the teacher to model ways to determine which types of

paragraphs to use, and how and when to use them. Writing shorter essays to begin with allows for more practice. By gradually adding length and complexity, students learn to consider the types of paragraphs that will best explain an idea or concept within an essay.

It is imperative to give students many opportunities to write several essays of the same type. Begin with reason essays and then example essays. Then mix reason and example paragraphs within an essay. Next, assign an essay with the theme "How to Use Structured Writing" to provide experience writing a process essay. Students' interests can also become topics for essay-writing practice. Explaining one's learning style or strengths provides opportunities to write classification essays, and explaining one's learning strengths and weaknesses is suitable for a compare and contrast essay. Writing many short essays of one specific type before moving on to the next more complex type provides writing practice that reinforces previous learning.

For further practice, model lessons requiring three different paragraph types to make up the body of an essay. For example, ask students to write a basic paragraph about what makes a student successful, or have them brainstorm behaviors and characteristics of successful students. From this paragraph or brainstorm, assign a five-paragraph essay that must include a reason paragraph, an example paragraph, and a process paragraph. Students must decide which quality or student behavior can best be explained by the different paragraph types required by the assignment. They choose the introductory and concluding methods individually. This activity emphasizes paragraph and essay structure, but it also allows room for a student to begin developing his or her individual voice. As students become more confident with essay structure, their writing becomes more original and self-assured.

The various essay webs and organizers are included on the CD-ROM. Follow the same procedure for each of the several essay types:

reason, example, process, classification, and compare and contrast.

Evaluation Rubric

Use the more complex Expository Essay Rubric to evaluate and validate student progress with each of the various types of essays. This rubric focuses on student aptitude in following and filling out the essay templates, including the essential elements of each individual paragraph. It also highlights writing mechanics and sentence structure. As the essays increase in difficulty, teacher expectations regarding sentence complexity should also increase. Content is assessed based on the strength, clarity, and appropriateness of the thesis/focus sentence, support topics, and elaborating remarks. Paragraph variety and development is also emphasized.

Expository Essay Rubric

STRUCTURE	EMERGING	DEVELOPING	PROFICIENT
Introduction	Introductory paragraph contains: ◆ Thesis/focus sentence	Introductory paragraph contains: ◆ Thesis/focus sentence ◆ Plan/sequence of support topics	Introductory paragraph contains: ◆ Thesis/focus sentence ◆ Plan/sequence of support topics ◆ Introductory comments ◆ Attention-getter
Body	Body contains at least three supporting paragraphs that: ◆ Relate to the thesis/focus sentence	Body contains at least three supporting paragraphs that: ◆ Develop the thesis/focus sentence ◆ Are presented in logical order	Body contains at least three supporting paragraphs that: ◆ Develop the thesis/focus sentence ◆ Are presented in logical order ◆ Use transition sentences to link paragraphs
Conclusion	Concluding paragraph contains: ◆ Reference to thesis/focus sentence	Concluding paragraph contains: ◆ Reference to thesis/focus sentence ◆ Summary of body paragraphs	Concluding paragraph contains: ◆ Reference to thesis/focus sentence ◆ Summary of body paragraphs ◆ Effective use of closing techniques/clincher
MECHANICS	EMERGING	DEVELOPING	PROFICIENT
Capitalization	Correct capitalization of: ◆ Sentences	Correct capitalization of: ◆ Sentences ◆ Proper nouns	Correct capitalization of: ◆ Sentences ◆ Proper nouns ◆ Titles ◆ Quotations
Punctuation	Correct use of: ◆ Sentence-ending punctuation	Correct use of: ◆ Sentence-ending punctuation ◆ Quotation marks	Correct use of: ◆ Sentence-ending punctuation ◆ Quotation marks ◆ Commas ◆ Apostrophes

Continued on next page

Expository Essay Rubric, continued

MECHANICS	EMERGING	DEVELOPING	PROFICIENT
Spelling	Spelling is: ◆ Correct enough to read ◆ Inconsistently checked with spelling checker	Spelling is: ◆ Correct ◆ Effectively checked with spelling checker ◆ Checked with text-to-speech feature	Spelling is: ◆ Correct ◆ Effectively checked with spelling checker ◆ Checked with text-to-speech feature ◆ Correct for homonyms and proper nouns
Sentence Structure	Sentences: ◆ Are structurally correct	Sentences: ◆ Are structurally correct ◆ Begin in various ways ◆ Contain diverse modifiers	Sentences: ◆ Are structurally correct ◆ Begin in various ways ◆ Contain diverse modifiers ◆ Vary in length ◆ Include compound and complex syntax

CONTENT	EMERGING	DEVELOPING	PROFICIENT
Thesis/Focus Sentence	Thesis/focus sentence is: ◆ Indirectly stated	Thesis/focus sentence is: ◆ Clearly stated ◆ Supportable	Thesis/focus sentence is: ◆ Clearly stated ◆ Supportable ◆ Important
Support Topics	At least three support topics that: ◆ Expand on the thesis/focus sentence	At least three support topics that: ◆ Expand on the thesis/focus sentence ◆ Are plausible	At least three support topics that: ◆ Expand on the thesis/focus sentence ◆ Are plausible ◆ Imaginatively link ideas
Facts/Elaboration	Facts and details in support paragraphs are: ◆ Relevant and appropriate	Facts and details in support paragraphs are: ◆ Relevant and appropriate ◆ Documented	Facts and details in support paragraphs are: ◆ Relevant and appropriate ◆ Documented ◆ Diverse
Paragraph Development	Paragraphs are: ◆ A specific type (intro, body, conclusion) ◆ Fully formed (topic sentence, supporting sentences, concluding sentence)	Paragraphs are: ◆ A specific type (intro, body, conclusion) ◆ Fully formed (topic sentence, supporting sentences, concluding sentence) ◆ Logically ordered	Paragraphs are: ◆ A specific type (intro, body, conclusion) ◆ Fully formed (topic sentence, supporting sentences, concluding sentence) ◆ Logically ordered ◆ Smoothly connected with appropriate transitions

Suggested Topics
for Expository Essays

Reason Essays
Why Vacations Are Great
The Benefits of School
    Uniforms
Too Much Homework

Example Essays
Successful Students
Ways I Am Smart
Learning Strengths and
    Weaknesses
Learning Modalities
School Sports

Classification Essays
Video Games
Television Shows
School Sports
Books
Music
Multiple Intelligences

Process Essays
How to Use Structured Writing
How to Be a Successful Student
Ways to Improve Study Skills
How to String a Lacrosse Stick
How to Do Homework

Compare and Contrast Essays
Learning Strengths and Weaknesses
Computers Versus Paper and Pencil
Reading With Books on Tape
Cats and Dogs

"Mixed" Essays *(The body of the essay comprises a mix of paragraph types)*

▶ **Successful Students**
First Body Paragraph; Reason: *Why success is important*
Second Body Paragraph; Example: *What determines success*
Third Body Paragraph; Process: *How to become a successful student*

▶ **Ways I Am Smart (Multiple Intelligences)**
First Body Paragraph; Example: *Student's strengths*
Second Body Paragraph; Classification: *Types of intelligence*
Third Body Paragraph; Compare and Contrast: *Learning strengths and
    difficulties*

▶ **Multimedia Presentations and Written Essays**
First Body Paragraph; Example: *Writers and the use of multimedia software*
Second Body Paragraph; Process: *How to create a multimedia presentation*
Third Body Paragraph; Compare and Contrast: *Written expression versus
    multimedia authoring*

Chapter 6

Persuasive Essays

Expository essays require beginning writers to come up with a main idea that announces the paper's theme. Persuasive essays, on the other hand, require authors to develop a thesis assertion on a meaningful subject. The writers must take a risk and develop an opinion about a topic based on their own research. Once students have successfully practiced writing the various expository essays, they are ready to compose persuasive essays.

The purpose of the persuasive essay is to present a definite opinion about a controversial issue and persuade the reader to feel likewise about the subject. Writers must clearly explain their opinions in positive terms and include compelling facts and reasons to support that point of view. The persuasive essay speaks with confidence, clarity, and sincerity. It addresses reasonable opposing arguments and points out their weaknesses. The strongest point is often saved for last in a persuasive essay to prove to skeptical readers they have something to benefit by assuming the same stance.

The persuasive essay contains an introductory paragraph that includes a thesis/focus sentence, three or more supporting body paragraphs, and a concluding paragraph. Students use the introductory paragraph to gain the reader's attention and identify the controversy. Each of the body paragraphs begins with the writer's position, followed by facts, reasons, and examples to support it. Rather than simply announcing the subject of the essay, students develop an opinion about the topic based on some research they have done. Opposing sides of the issue and their weaknesses are cited, solutions proposed, and the writer's outlook is confirmed in the conclusion.

Objectives

1. Students will write a persuasive essay using an introductory paragraph, three supporting paragraphs, and a concluding paragraph.

2. Students will use the steps of the Structured Writing II process to plan, write, edit, format, and publish a persuasive essay.

3. Students will use the sequential editing steps in the Structured Writing process. They will use text-to-speech features to read and listen while checking the writing content, capitalization, punctuation, word usage, and spelling. They will make revisions to increase sentence complexity and use a thesaurus to enhance vocabulary and eliminate overused words.

Materials Needed

Structured Writing II CD-ROM

- Persuasive Essay Web
- Persuasive Essay Organizer

Inspiration 6.0 or 7.0

Word processing program

Posters

- ◆ Persuasive Essay Web
- ◆ Editing Steps (chapter 1)
- ◆ Possible Conclusions (chapter 3)
- ◆ Five-Paragraph Essay Planner (chapter 4)

Essential Elements

The Structured Writing II process teaches students to write a persuasive essay using:

1. An **introductory paragraph** identifying a controversial issue
2. Three **supporting paragraphs** to:
   a. State the writer's position
   b. Raise possible opposing views
   c. Provide possible solutions
3. A **concluding paragraph** to reaffirm the writer's position

Color Codes

- ◆ White for the essay title
- ◆ Blue for paragraph types
- ◆ Yellow for topic and concluding sentences
- ◆ Green for supporting sentences
- ◆ Pink for details and elaboration

The Structured Writing II Process

Planning step: Outline the essay.

Writing step: Expand ideas into sentences. Organize sentences into paragraphs.

Editing step: Edit and revise one paragraph at a time.

Formatting step: Create a draft in essay format.

Publishing step: Print the final copy.

The Editing Process

1. Open the organizer file.
2. Use text-to-speech to read and listen to each sentence, one at a time, to check content. Edit and revise.
3. Check capitalization.
4. Check punctuation.
5. Check for homonyms and misused words.
6. Run a spelling checker.
7. Read and listen to changes using text-to-speech.
8. Save changes.
9. Print in color or print and highlight by hand.
10. Submit to a proofreader for review.
11. Make any necessary changes suggested by the proofreader.
12. Give to the teacher for feedback and approval.

The Persuasive Essay Process

The Planning Step

Students begin the planning step by opening the Persuasive Essay Web template. The template is on the CD-ROM accompanying this book. It is also reproduced in poster form on the following foldout page. This template helps students plan the essay using facts and reasons to persuade readers to adopt their point of view on a controversial issue. The color code and text identify the essential parts of the essay (title, introductory paragraph, three supporting paragraphs, and a concluding paragraph) and the essential elements of each paragraph (topic sentence, supporting sentences, and concluding sentence). The Notes feature of Inspiration provides extra scaffolding for struggling students.

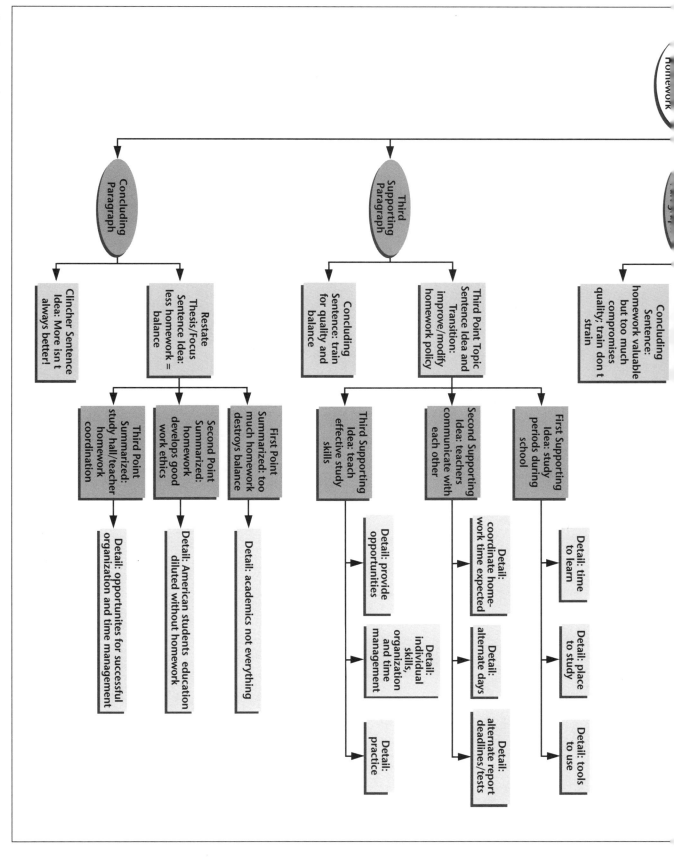

homework

Concluding Paragraph

Clincher Sentence Idea: More isn't always better!

Restate Thesis/Focus Sentence Idea: less homework = balance

Third Point Summarized: study hall/teacher homework coordination

Detail: opportunites for successful organization and time management

Second Point Summarized: homework develops good work ethics

Detail: American students' education diluted without homework

First Point Summarized: too much homework destroys balance

Detail: academics not everything

Third Supporting Paragraph

Concluding Sentence: train for quality and balance

Third Point Topic Sentence Idea and Transition: improve/modify homework policy

Third Supporting Idea: teach effective study skills

Detail: provide opportunities

Detail: individual skills, organization and time management

Detail: practice

Second Supporting Idea: teachers communicate with each other

Detail: coordinate home-work time expected

Detail: alternate days

Detail: alternate report deadlines/tests

First Supporting Idea: study periods during school

Detail: time to learn

Detail: place to study

Detail: tools to use

Concluding Sentence: homework valuable but too much compromises quality; train don't strain

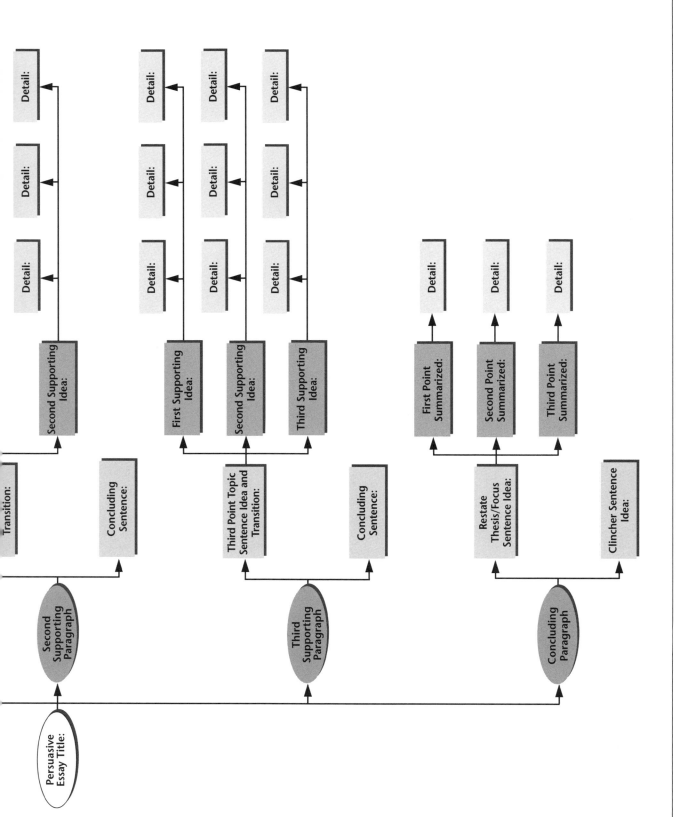

Persuasive Essay Web

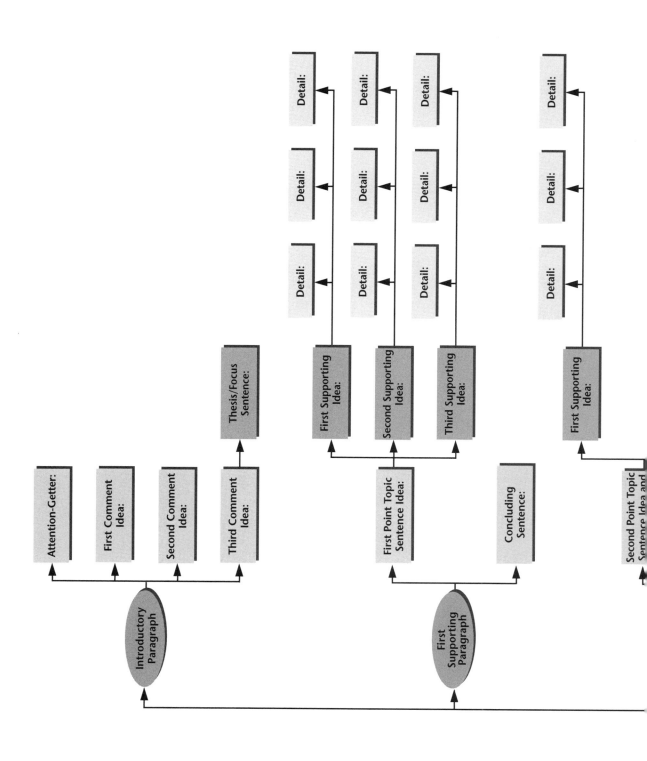

Attention-Getter:

First Comment Idea:

Second Comment Idea:

Third Comment Idea:

Thesis/Focus Sentence:

Introductory Paragraph

First Point Topic Sentence Idea:

First Supporting Idea:

Second Supporting Idea:

Third Supporting Idea:

Detail:

Detail:

Detail:

Concluding Sentence:

First Supporting Paragraph

Second Point Topic Sentence Idea and

First Supporting Idea:

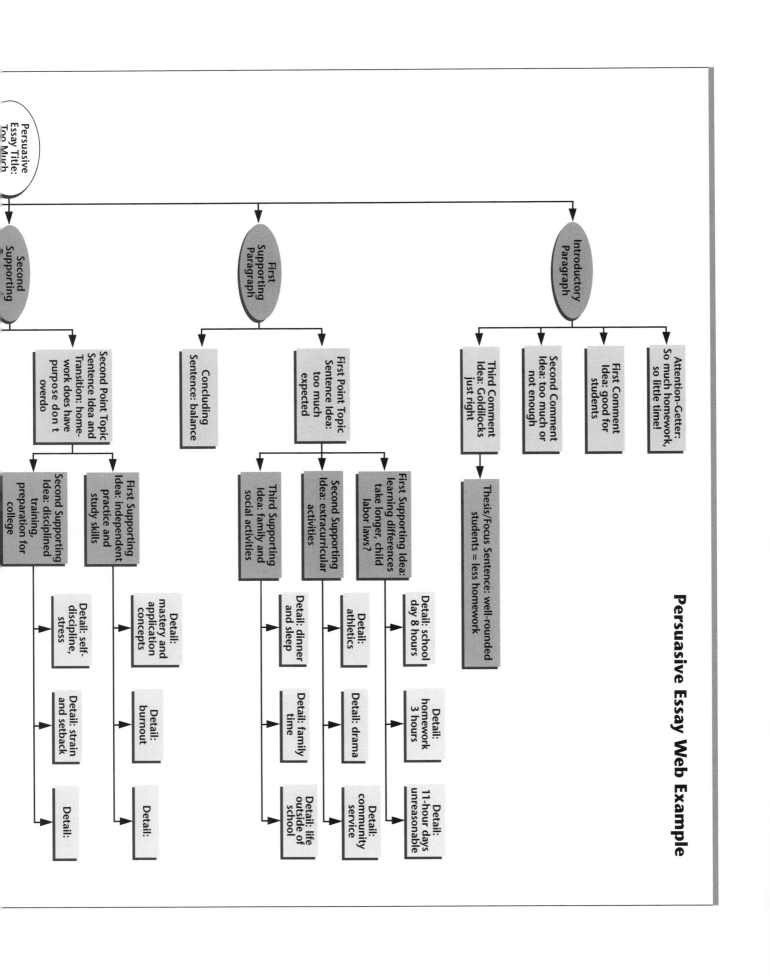

Persuasive Essay Web Example

Persuasive Essay Title: Too Much

Introductory Paragraph

- Attention-Getter: So much homework, so little time!
- First Comment Idea: good for students
- Second Comment Idea: too much or not enough
- Third Comment Idea: Goldilocks just right
  - Thesis/Focus Sentence: well-rounded students = less homework

First Supporting Paragraph

- First Point Topic Sentence Idea: too much expected
  - First Supporting Idea: learning differences take longer, child labor laws?
    - Detail: school day 8 hours
    - Detail: homework 3 hours
    - Detail: 11-hour days unreasonable
  - Second Supporting Idea: extracurricular activities
    - Detail: athletics
    - Detail: drama
    - Detail: community service
  - Third Supporting Idea: family and social activities
    - Detail: dinner and sleep
    - Detail: family time
    - Detail: life outside of school
- Concluding Sentence: balance

Second Supporting

- Second Point Topic Sentence Idea and Transition: home-work does have purpose don t overdo
  - First Supporting Idea: independent practice and study skills
    - Detail: mastery and application concepts
    - Detail: burnout
    - Detail:
  - Second Supporting Idea: disciplined training, preparation for college
    - Detail: self-discipline, stress
    - Detail: strain and setback
    - Detail:

The Five-Paragraph Essay Planner poster in chapter 4 provides an outline for guidance through the planning process. Following are directions for completing the planning step. Model the lesson with the persuasive essay topic "Too Much Homework."

1. Students open the Persuasive Essay Web. The white box in the web indicates the place for the essay title. The blue ovals identify the paragraph types within the essay. The yellow boxes are for topic and concluding sentence ideas within each paragraph. The green boxes signify supporting sentence ideas. The pink boxes are for the details about the supporting ideas.

2. Students type key words and short phrases in the Persuasive Essay Web to represent their ideas. Structure cues indicate the specific information required and where it goes. (The foldout page in this chapter shows the Persuasive Essay Web on one side and the Persuasive Essay Web with the homework ideas filled in on the other side.) **Reinforce the distinction between organizing ideas by outlining and actually writing sentences.** It is important that students organize their ideas for the essay as a whole prior to the writing step. In a persuasive essay, the body paragraphs require specific information in a particular order. The words and phrases in the web will be converted to an outline to use as a guide for writing each paragraph later in the writing step.

3. When all the boxes are completed, students convert the web into a color-coded outline by selecting the Outline option in Inspiration. If changes need to be made in the order of the paragraphs, it is easier to rearrange them in the outline format. Students run the spelling checker and save the Persuasive Essay Outline as "essay title.outline" in the appropriate folder or directory. Figure 35 shows the Persuasive Essay Outline template and Figure 36 shows

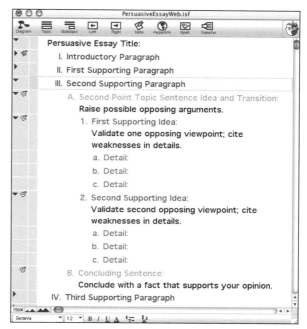

Figure 34. The Persuasive Essay Outline template with only the second supporting paragraph displayed in detail.

the Persuasive Essay Outline with the homework ideas filled in.

4. Some students may be overwhelmed or distracted by the entire essay while working on individual paragraphs. To simplify the visuals, simply close the topic windows in the outline format and let students view only one paragraph at a time while they write. Figure 34 shows an outline with just the Second Supporting Paragraph showing in full detail.

5. When students are ready to print their outlines, they must first go to View in the main menu, then to Notes, and check Hide All to hide the notes on the outline. Then, students go to File in the main menu, scroll to Page Setup, and uncheck Hidden Notes. These steps will keep the notes from appearing on the printed document. See chapter 3, Figures 9 and 10, for more details.

6. Students print the color-coded outline or print it and highlight it by hand.

Persuasive Essay Outline

Persuasive Essay Title:

I. Introductory Paragraph: *Introduce a controversial issue.*

   A. Attention-Getter:

   B. First Comment Idea: *Give background information.*

   C. Second Comment Idea: *Acknowledge opposing argument.*

   D. Third Comment Idea:

      1. Thesis/Focus Sentence: *Clearly state your opinion positively: value, fact, or policy.*

II. First Supporting Paragraph

   A. First Point Topic Sentence Idea: *State your position.*

      1. First Supporting Idea: *Provide first fact and evidence.*

         a. Detail:

         b. Detail:

         c. Detail:

      2. Second Supporting Idea: *Provide second fact and evidence.*

         a. Detail:

         b. Detail:

         c. Detail:

      3. Third Supporting Idea: *Provide third fact and evidence.*

         a. Detail:

         b. Detail:

         c. Detail:

   B. Concluding Sentence:

III. Second Supporting Paragraph

   A. Second Point Topic Sentence Idea and Transition: *Raise possible opposing arguments.*

      1. First Supporting Idea: *Validate first opposing viewpoint; cite weaknesses in details.*

         a. Detail:

         b. Detail:

         c. Detail:

      2. Second Supporting Idea: *Validate second opposing viewpoint; cite weaknesses in details.*

         a. Detail:

         b. Detail:

         c. Detail:

   B. Concluding Sentence: *Conclude with a fact that supports your opinion.*

IV. Third Supporting Paragraph

   A. Third Point Topic Sentence Idea and Transition: *Provide a reasonable solution to the controversy.*

      1. First Supporting Idea:

         a. Detail:

         b. Detail:

         c. Detail:

      2. Second Supporting Idea:

         a. Detail:

         b. Detail:

         c. Detail:

      3. Third Supporting Idea:

         a. Detail:

         b. Detail:

         c. Detail:

   B. Concluding Sentence:

V. Concluding Paragraph

   A. Restate Thesis/Focus Sentence Idea: *Reaffirm your opinion.*

      1. First Point Summarized:

         a. Detail:

      2. Second Point Summarized:

         a. Detail:

      3. Third Point Summarized:

         a. Detail:

   B. Clincher Sentence Idea: *Leave readers with a final thought.*

Figure 35. The complete Persuasive Essay Outline template.

7. Students give the outline to the teacher for review.

The teacher checks for content, order, and completeness to give feedback to the students before they begin the writing step. Reassured that they are on the right track, students use the outline to guide their writing in the next step.

Example Persuasive Essay Outline

Persuasive Essay Title: Too Much Homework

I. **Introductory Paragraph:**

   A. **Attention-Getter:** So much homework, so little time!

   B. **First Comment:** good for students

   C. **Second Comment:** too much or not enough

   D. **Third Comment:** Goldilocks just right

      1. **Thesis/Focus Sentence:** well-rounded students = less homework

II. **First Supporting Paragraph**

   A. **First Point Topic Sentence Idea:** too much expected

      1. **First Supporting Idea:** learning differences takes longer, child labor laws?

         a. **Detail:** school day 8 hours

         b. **Detail:** homework 3 hours

         c. **Detail:** 11-hour days unreasonable

      2. **Second Supporting Idea:** extracurricular activities

         a. **Detail:** athletics

         b. **Detail:** drama

         c. **Detail:** community service

      3. **Third Supporting Idea:** family and social activities

         a. **Detail:** dinner and sleep

         b. **Detail:** family time

         c. **Detail:** life outside of school

   B. **Concluding Sentence:** balance

III. **Second Supporting Paragraph**

   A. **Second Point Topic Sentence Idea and Transition:** homework does have purpose—don't overdo

      1. **First Supporting Idea:** Independent practice and study skills

         a. **Detail:** mastery and application concepts

         b. **Detail:** burnout

      2. **Second Supporting Idea:** disciplined training, preparation for college

         a. **Detail:** self-discipline, stress

         b. **Detail:** strain and setback

   B. **Concluding Sentence:** homework valuable but too much compromises quality; train don't strain

IV. **Third Supporting Paragraph**

   A. **Third Point Topic Sentence Idea and Transition:** improve/modify homework policy

      1. **First Supporting Idea:** study periods during school

         a. **Detail:** time to learn

         b. **Detail:** place to study

         c. **Detail:** tools to use

      2. **Second Supporting Idea:** teachers communicate with each other

         a. **Detail:** coordinate homework time expected

         b. **Detail:** alternate days

         c. **Detail:** alternate report deadlines/tests

      3. **Third Supporting Idea:** teach effective study skills

         a. **Detail:** provide opportunities

         b. **Detail:** individual skills—organization and time management

         c. **Detail:** practice

   B. **Concluding Sentence:** train for quality and balance

V. **Concluding Paragraph**

   A. **Restate Thesis/Focus Sentence Idea:** less homework = balance

      1. **First Point Summarized:** too much homework destroys balance

         a. **Detail:** academics not everything

      2. **Second Point Summarized:** homework develops good work ethics

         a. **Detail:** American students' education diluted without homework

      3. **Third Point Summarized:** study hall/teacher homework coordination

         a. **Detail:** opportunities for successful organization and time management

   B. **Clincher Sentence Idea:** More isn't always better!

Figure 36. The essay outline filled in with a student's ideas about homework.

The Writing Step

Compose the Introductory Paragraph

Students begin the persuasive essay writing step by opening the Persuasive Essay Organizer in the appropriate word processing program found on the accompanying CD-ROM. Using the color-coded outline to guide their writing, students begin writing the introductory paragraph with a forthright and precise thesis/focus sentence that clearly states the controversial issue and the writer's opinion about it. Students use various introduction techniques explained previously to capture the reader's attention and provide background information about the issue. They develop the initial paragraph using related comments and details in complete sentences.

1. Students introduce and give background information on a controversial issue with the **attention-getter** and **introductory comments**. They write the **thesis/focus sentence** to clearly and positively state their position on the issue.

2. Text cues indicate the appropriate information, and the color code reinforces the paragraph structure. Students attend to the purpose of their essays and set the tone of the opening, choosing colorful adjectives and strong verbs to "hook" the reader (Figure 37).

3. When the introductory paragraph sentences are complete, the students save the paragraph as "essay title.organizer" in the proper folder or directory.

Compose the Supporting Paragraphs

Students continue to use the same color-coded Persuasive Essay Organizer to write the body of the essay, writing supporting paragraphs one at a time. They make sure sentences are complete and clearly express what they intend to communicate. Each paragraph will be edited and revised in the editing step, one sentence at a time.

Example Persuasive Essay Organizer— Introductory Paragraph

Persuasuve Essay by: Student Name

Essay Title: Too Much Homework!

Introductory Paragraph

Attention-Getter: So much homework, so little time!

First Comment: Teachers, students, and parents agree that independent practice, a.k.a. homework, is necessary for learners to rehearse their academic skills.

Second Comment: Nevertheless, too much homework, or not enough, is the question of the day.

Third Comment: We don't need Goldilocks to determine how much homework is just right.

Thesis/Focus Sentence: Students require less academic homework to become well-rounded students and citizens.

Figure 37. A filled-in introductory paragraph.

First Supporting Paragraph: The writer's opinion is discussed in the first supporting paragraph (Figure 38). Authors can use evidence, statistics, expert testimony, observations, predictions, and comparisons to convincingly support their stance.

1. Students continue to use their outlines to guide their composition of supporting and detail sentences. Each paragraph will be refined in the editing step.

2. Teachers continue to direct students to use adjective and adverb modifiers and prepositional phrases to clarify their prose. Students are instructed to combine simple sentences into compound sentences, to use complex sentences, and to vary sentence structure. They are encouraged to consult a thesaurus to eliminate overused words, improve vocabulary, and enhance the intricacy of their written expression. Students use appropriate transition words in the green structure sentences to indicate the main points within each paragraph.

3. Once the sentences in the first supporting paragraph are completed, the students add

---

Example Persuasive Essay Organizer—First Supporting Paragraph

Persuasive Essay by: Student Name
Essay Title: Too Much Homework!

First Supporting Paragraph—Writer's Position

Topic Sentence: The excessive time it takes to complete homework assignments is crippling students' personal development.

First Supporting Sentence: *First of all*, students with learning differences take longer to complete homework assignments.

Detail: They spend eight hours in school, five days a week.

Detail: Then their homework consumes two to three more hours in an evening.

Detail: Eleven-hour workdays are unreasonable for children.

Second Supporting Sentence: *Second*, students are encouraged to participate in extracurricular activities and need time to do so.

Detail: Athletic programs provide students with physically and socially stimulating activities that usually occur after school hours.

Detail: Students active in drama must spend extra hours at rehearsals and during performances.

Detail: Involvement in community service also requires many hours in addition to class time.

Third Supporting Sentence: *Finally*, family and social commitments require daily attention.

Detail: Students connecting with family members at dinnertime tend to generally do better in school than those who do not.

Detail: Family time offers students the time to restore their energy and to relax.

Detail: Friendships and activities not related to school ought to be honored and valued with participation time.

Concluding Sentence: Balance is the goal.

Figure 38. Transition words are underlined and italicized.

it to the organizer by saving it as "essay title.organizer" in the proper folder or directory. They then move on to the second body paragraph, and then the third.

Second Supporting Paragraph: The second supporting paragraph in the persuasive essay identifies possible arguments against the writer's opinion (Figure 39). Students should yield to the validity of a reliable argument because acknowledging another perspective oftentimes makes one's opinion more convincing.

1. Students write topic sentences with transitions to unite the separate paragraphs in the essay.

2. Students state the possible arguments to their position and cite the weaknesses in the detail sentences. Students mention fewer arguments against their position.

3. They add each paragraph to the organizer one at a time. (The entire essay organizer will be arranged into a draft in the formatting step.)

Third Supporting Paragraph: The third supporting paragraph in the body of the persuasive essay provides a reasonable solution to the controversy (Figure 40). The topic sentence requires an appropriate transition, and the supporting evidence can be reasons, examples, statistics, and the like. It is best to use appropriate qualifiers to more easily support one's opinions.

Compose the Concluding Paragraph

Teachers repeat the essential elements of the concluding paragraph: a topic sentence reaffirming the writer's point of view from the thesis/focus sentence using a specific method (see the Possible Conclusions poster at the end of chapter 3), three supporting sentences referring to each of the three body paragraphs, one or more details about each, and a clincher sentence.

Students use the concluding paragraph section in the Persuasive Essay Organizer to expand their closing ideas into sentences, one at a time (Figure 41). Text cues indicate the required

Example Persuasive Essay Organizer—Second Supporting Paragraph

Persuasive Essay by: Student Name

Essay Title: Too Much Homework!

Second Supporting Paragraph— Opposing Arguments

Topic Sentence and Transition: *In spite of the excessive time it requires,* homework in itself is valuable and does have a purpose.

First Supporting Sentence: *For instance,* it provides students with the opportunities to practice and develop study skills.

Detail: Students must master and be able to apply concepts learned in the real world.

Detail: Too much time spent on mastery causes burnout when students are overwhelmed with academic time commitments.

Second Supporting Sentence: *Also,* homework provides necessary training and self-discipline for college-bound students as well as students bound for the work force.

Detail: Homework overload causes stress.

Detail: Stress causes strain that often results in setbacks rather than progress.

Concluding Sentence: Homework is valuable but too much compromises quality: train, don't strain.

Figure 39. Transition words are underlined and italicized.

Example Persuasive Essay Organizer—Third Supporting Paragraph

Persuasive Essay by: Student Name

Essay Title: Too Much Homework!

Third Supporting Paragraph— Solution to Controversy

Topic Sentence and Transition: *Considering the problems and usefulness of homework assignments,* it is clear that the current homework policy must be modified to allow students to efficiently handle appropriate amounts of homework.

First Supporting Sentence: *One solution* is to add a study period to the school day.

Detail: It would provide time for students to do class assignments during their workday.

Detail: Study sessions would supply the appropriate places to study without the distractions of home.

Detail: Materials and tools needed to complete assignments would be readily available in the school study hall environment.

Second Supporting Sentence: *Another resolution* is for teachers to communicate with each other about their assignments.

Detail: They could coordinate homework assignments to fit students' expected study time.

Detail: Instructors might assign class work every other day.

Detail: Alternating report deadlines and test dates would assist students to manage their study time more efficiently.

Third Supporting Sentence: *In addition,* teachers could directly teach independent study skills.

Detail: The study hall would provide the opportunity for the students to learn specific study strategies.

Detail: Individual pupils would become aware of their individual needs regarding organization and time management proficiency.

Detail: Study skills training provides practice time.

Concluding Sentence: Students must be trained to produce quality assignments and maintain balance in their lives.

Figure 40. Transition words are underlined and italicized.

Example Persuasive Essay Organizer—Concluding Paragraph

Persuasive Essay by: Student Name

Essay Title: Too Much Homework!

**Concluding Paragraph—
Reaffirm Writer's Opinion**

Restate Thesis/Focus Sentence: Less homework is the key to balance for students.

First Point Summarized: Too much homework destroys balance.

Detail: Academics are not everything.

Second Point Summarized: Quality homework completion leads to a good work ethic.

Detail: American students' education is weak without homework.

Third Point Summarized: Study halls and coordination of homework assignments are two possible solutions to the homework controversy.

Detail: Successful organization and effective time management are key skills to learn.

Clincher Sentence: More isn't always better—especially when it comes to homework!

Figure 41. An organizer with its concluding paragraph filled in.

information, and the color code reinforces the paragraph structure.

1. Students take a stand when ending their essays.

2. Students consider their audience and purpose for writing the essay, the tone they have established, and the points made to determine a memorable conclusion.

Concluding paragraphs answer any questions left unanswered in the body paragraphs, summarize the main points, or emphasize the special importance of one of the main points. Conclusion paragraphs restate the thesis/focus sentence or primary message, and say something that will keep the readers thinking about the subject. Leaving readers with a strong image, or perhaps a bit of wit, effectively "wraps up" a composition (see chapter 3, the Concluding Paragraph Lesson).

When the concluding paragraph sentences are complete, the students add it to the organizer by saving it as "essay title.organizer" in the appropriate folder or directory.

The Editing Step

Students edit one paragraph at a time in the Persuasive Essay Organizer using the Structured Writing process. Once the initial purpose, structure, sequence, and information are

established, students revise sentences within the paragraphs to refine the essay. Students check capitalization, punctuation, homonyms, and spelling in the specific order described in the Structured Writing editing process, one paragraph at a time. Encourage students to refer to the Editing Steps poster (chapter 1) to help them through the process.

1. Students open the saved organizer, "essay title.organizer."

2. Students read and listen to each paragraph, one sentence at a time, using the text-to-speech features to check the content of their writing beginning with the introductory paragraph. Each individual paragraph is edited and revised as a whole within the entire multi-paragraph essay.

◆ Students add, delete, rearrange, and change words until the sentences sound "right" and communicate the intended meaning. Students should vary sentence structure, use different kinds of sentences, and consult a thesaurus to eliminate overused words and increase the complexity of their vocabulary.

◆ They specifically check for appropriate transition sentences between the second and third body paragraphs.

3. Students check capitalization.

4. Students check punctuation.

5. Students check word usage, including homonyms and misused words.

6. Students check spelling.

7. Students read and listen to changes using text-to-speech.

8. Students save their edited essay organizers in the appropriate folder or directory as "essay title.organizer." Each individual paragraph is edited one at a time and saved in the essay organizer. Each subsequent edited paragraph is added by saving it and thereby replacing the previous organizer.

9. Students print the edited essay organizer in color or print it and highlight it by hand.

10. Students give the document to a proofreader for review.

11. Students make any necessary changes suggested by the proofreader.

12. Students submit the document to the teacher for feedback and approval.

Teachers assess the sentences and paragraphs in the organizer for appropriate content, proper syntax, and sentence variation. Once edited organizers are approved, students move to the formatting step.

Students have now edited the individual paragraph organizers within the essay, one at a time. These paragraphs are ready to be formatted into the complete essay.

The Formatting Step

In this step, students prepare the document for publishing. The color code remains to reinforce paragraph structure within the essay.

1. Students put the required heading on the document, such as their name and the date.

2. Students delete the structure cues and place the sentences in proper paragraph form as learned in the Structured Writing process, one paragraph at a time, beginning with the introductory paragraph. They maintain appropriate spacing after ending punctuation (one or two spaces) and between lines (single, one and a half, or double spacing). The same procedure is used for each of the remaining paragraphs.

3. Students center the essay title and indent topic sentences.

4. Students read and listen to the entire essay, paying attention to the flow of ideas.

5. Students save the document as "essay title.draft" in the proper folder or directory.

6. When satisfied, students print the document in color or print it and highlight it by hand.

7. Students give the draft to a proofreader for review.

The essay draft in Figure 42 is based on the writing of three eighth graders with learning disabilities. They had about two years of experience working with the Structured Writing process, and this was what they came up with for their persuasive essay assignment. They wrote about the homework policy at their school. They wanted a study hall period included in the day and teachers to coordinate assignments on "game days" so they could participate in after-school sports programs.

The Publishing Step

When students receive approved essay drafts, the writing process is complete except for removing the color code and printing a final copy.

1. Students consider the proofreader's suggestions and make the necessary corrections.

Student Name

Date

Too Much Homework!

So much homework, so little time! Teachers, students, and parents agree that independent practice, a.k.a. homework, is necessary for learners to rehearse their academic skills. Nevertheless, too much homework, or not enough, is the question of the day. We don't need Goldilocks to determine how much homework is just right. Students require less academic homework to become well-rounded students and citizens.

The excessive time it takes to complete homework assignments is crippling students' personal development. First of all, students with learning differences take longer to complete homework assignments. They spend eight hours in school, five days a week. Then their homework consumes two to three more hours in an evening. Eleven-hour workdays are unreasonable for children. Second, students are encouraged to participate in extracurricular activities and need time to do so. Athletic programs provide students with physically and socially stimulating activities that usually occur after school hours. Students active in drama must spend extra hours at rehearsals and during performances. Involvement in community service also requires many hours in addition to class time. Finally, family and social commitments require daily attention. Students connecting with family members at dinnertime tend to generally do better in school than those who do not. Family time offers students the time to restore their energy and to relax. Friendships and activities not related to school ought to be honored and valued with participation time. Balance is the goal.

In spite of the excessive time it requires, homework in itself is valuable and does have a purpose. For instance, it provides students with the opportunities to practice and develop study skills. Students must master and be able to apply concepts learned in the real world. Too much time spent on mastery causes burnout when students are overwhelmed with academic time commitments. Second, homework provides necessary training and self-discipline for college-bound students as well as students bound for the work force. Homework overload causes stress. Stress causes strain that oftentimes results in setbacks rather than progress. Homework is valuable, but too much compromises quality: train, don't strain.

Considering the problems and usefulness of homework assignments, it is clear the homework policy at school must be modified to allow students to efficiently handle appropriate amounts of homework. One solution is to add a study period to the school day. It would provide time for students to do class assignments during their workday. Study sessions would supply the appropriate places to study without the distractions of home. Materials and tools needed to complete assignments would be readily available in the school study hall environment. Another resolution is for teachers to communicate with each other about their assignments. They could coordinate homework assignments to fit students' expected study time. Instructors might assign class work every other day. Alternating report deadlines and test dates would assist students to manage their study time more efficiently. In addition, teachers could directly teach independent study skills. The study hall would provide the opportunity for the students to learn specific study strategies. Individual pupils would become aware of their individual needs regarding organization and time management proficiency. Study skills training provides practice time. Students must be trained to produce quality assignments and maintain balance in their lives.

Less homework is the key to balance for students. Too much homework destroys balance. Academics are not everything. Quality homework completion does lead to a good work ethic. American students' education is weak without homework. Study halls and teacher coordination of homework assignments are two possible solutions to the homework controversy. Successful organization and effective time management are key skills to learn. More isn't always better—especially when it comes to homework!

Figure 42. A complete persuasive essay draft.

When any changes are made, students should reread and run another spelling check before resubmitting to a proofreader.

2. Students then change the text color to black.

3. They save the document in the appropriate folder or directory as "essay title.final copy."

4. Students print a final copy in black.

5. Students submit to the teacher a complete packet containing the outline, organizer, draft, and final copy.

Summary

The persuasive essay is a step up from the expository essay because it requires students to become informed about a controversial issue, consider surrounding facts and opinions, make decisions, take a stand, and support it with evidence that persuades the reader of their perspective. Individual paragraphs are combined into one complex document that includes:

- An **introductory paragraph** that identifies a controversial issue

- **Three supporting paragraphs t**hat state the writer's position, raise possible opposing views, and provide possible solutions

- A **concluding paragraph** that reaffirms the writer's position

In Structured Writing II, teachers emphasize content and complexity while the built-in structure of the Structured Writing process reinforces the essential elements of the specific essays that students are composing. Persuasive essays require a lot of thinking, planning, and organizing; students have to learn as much as they can about an issue, care about it, and form an opinion that can be supported and expanded in a compelling argument. For practice, propose "hot" topics: the school's

homework policy, school uniforms, and instant messaging are subjects that reveal opinionated students! Individual student voices emerge from their persuasive essays. While the Structured Writing II process emphasizes structure and logical sequencing, once students are confident with this structure, it frees them to focus on generating strong, persuasive, and ingenious arguments for their position.

Evaluation Rubric

The rubric for the persuasive essay focuses on student aptitude in writing an informative and persuasive paper that takes a particular point of view on a controversial topic. It evaluates the extent to which students followed and filled out the essay template to identify the controversy, impart an opinion, address opposing arguments, and provide possible solutions. Writing mechanics, sentence structure, and use of technology to independently and accurately edit the essay are also assessed. Content, however, should be the focus of evaluation when looking at a persuasive essay: the manner in which the thesis/focus sentence presents the controversy, the relevancy of the evidence cited, and the organization and logical arrangement of the individual paragraphs.

Persuasive Essay Rubric

STRUCTURE	EMERGING	DEVELOPING	PROFICIENT
Introduction	Introductory paragraph contains a thesis/focus sentence that: ◆ Identifies the controversy	Introductory paragraph contains a thesis/focus sentence that: ◆ Identifies the controversy ◆ Is opinion-based	Introductory paragraph contains a thesis/focus sentence that: ◆ Identifies the controversy ◆ Is opinion-based ◆ Is verifiable
Body	Body contains at least three supporting paragraphs that: ◆ Relate to the thesis/focus sentence	Body contains at least three supporting paragraphs that: ◆ Support writer's position ◆ Address opposing sides ◆ Provide possible solutions	Body contains at least three supporting paragraphs that: ◆ Support writer's position ◆ Address opposing sides ◆ Provide possible solutions ◆ Present facts/evidence ◆ Use effective transitions
Conclusion	Concluding paragraph contains: ◆ Reference to thesis/focus sentence	Concluding paragraph contains: ◆ Reference to thesis/focus sentence ◆ Summary of support topics	Concluding paragraph contains: ◆ Reference to thesis/focus sentence ◆ Summary of support topics ◆ Effective use of closing techniques/clincher

MECHANICS	EMERGING	DEVELOPING	PROFICIENT
Capitalization	Correct capitalization of: ◆ Sentences	Correct capitalization of: ◆ Sentences ◆ Proper nouns	Correct capitalization of: ◆ Sentences ◆ Proper nouns ◆ Titles ◆ Quotations
Punctuation	Correct use of: ◆ Sentence-ending punctuation	Correct use of: ◆ Sentence-ending punctuation ◆ Quotation marks	Correct use of: ◆ Sentence-ending punctuation ◆ Quotation marks ◆ Commas ◆ Apostrophes
Spelling	Spelling is: ◆ Correct enough to read ◆ Inconsistently checked with spelling checker	Spelling is: ◆ Correct ◆ Effectively checked with spelling checker ◆ Checked with text-to-speech feature	Spelling is: ◆ Correct ◆ Effectively checked with spelling checker ◆ Checked with text-to-speech feature ◆ Correct for homonyms and proper nouns

Continued on next page

Persuasive Essay Rubric, continued

MECHANICS	EMERGING	DEVELOPING	PROFICIENT
Sentence Structure	Sentences: ◆ Are structurally correct	Sentences: ◆ Are structurally correct ◆ Begin in various ways ◆ Contain diverse modifiers ◆ Include appropriate transition words	Sentences: ◆ Are structurally correct ◆ Begin in various ways ◆ Contain diverse modifiers ◆ Include appropriate transition words ◆ Vary in length ◆ Include compound and complex syntax

CONTENT	EMERGING	DEVELOPING	PROFICIENT
Thesis/Focus Sentence	Thesis/focus sentence: ◆ Identifies controversy	Thesis/focus sentence: ◆ Identifies controversy ◆ Is explicit ◆ Is opinion-based	Thesis/focus sentence: ◆ Identifies controversy ◆ Is explicit ◆ Is opinion-based ◆ Is verifiable ◆ Is important
Supporting Paragraphs	At least three supporting paragraphs that: ◆ Relate to the thesis/focus sentence	At least three supporting paragraphs that: ◆ Support the writer's position with facts and evidence ◆ Address opposing arguments and cite their weaknesses ◆ Provide possible solutions to the controversy	At least three supporting paragraphs that: ◆ Support the writer's position with facts and evidence ◆ Address opposing arguments and cite their weaknesses ◆ Provide possible solutions to the controversy ◆ Use effective transitions
Facts/Evidence	Supporting evidence is: ◆ Relevant	Supporting evidence is: ◆ Relevant ◆ Documented ◆ Convincing	Supporting evidence is: ◆ Relevant ◆ Documented ◆ Convincing ◆ Reliable
Paragraph Development	Paragraphs are: ◆ A specific type (intro, body, conclusion) ◆ Fully formed (topic sentence, supporting sentences, concluding sentence)	Paragraphs are: ◆ A specific type (intro, body, conclusion) ◆ Fully formed (topic sentence, supporting sentences, concluding sentence) ◆ Sequentially ordered (following template)	Paragraphs are: ◆ A specific type (intro, body, conclusion) ◆ Fully formed (topic sentence, supporting sentences, concluding sentence) ◆ Sequentially ordered (following template) ◆ Smoothly connected with appropriate transitions
Style	Ideas are: ◆ Presented in the writer's own words	Ideas are: ◆ Presented in the writer's own words ◆ Explicit and clear	Ideas are: ◆ Presented in the writer's own words ◆ Explicit and clear ◆ Expressed by specific nouns and strong verbs ◆ Clearly original

Chapter 7

Book Reports

Students familiar with writing the various types of expository essays and persuasive essays are ready to compose book reports. Instruction for writing book reports follows the same process used for writing essays.

The Structured Writing II book report requires students to state a reaction to, or opinion of, a book they have read, and support it with particulars and details. This lesson uses a traditional essay form starting with an introductory (information) paragraph, supporting paragraphs (the body), and a concluding (opinion) paragraph. The four main parts of a book are identified and discussed: the story plot, the characters, the setting, and the theme. Structured Writing II book reports are divided into the following three types according to their complexity and genres.

◆ **Basic book report:** employs three basic paragraphs that introduce the main characters, explain the overall idea and plot, and give a personal opinion of the literature.

◆ **Biography book report:** requires students to explain their perspective of the person, providing personal information that includes family and educational background in the information paragraph. Another paragraph explains the person's significance and accomplishments, and a final paragraph gives an opinion of the book.

◆ **Expanded book report:** provides information about the book, discusses

characterization and plot, and gives an opinion or a recommendation. This is the most complex type of book report.

The basic book report will be the model for this chapter. Use the same Structured Writing II process to teach students to write the more complex book reports, as shown later in this chapter.

Objectives

1. Students will write a three-paragraph basic book report using an information paragraph, a plot summary paragraph, and an opinion paragraph.

2. Students will use the steps of the Structured Writing II process to plan, write, edit, format, and publish a three-paragraph book report.

3. Students will use the sequential editing steps in the Structured Writing process. They will use text-to-speech features to read and listen while checking their writing content, capitalization, and punctuation. They will run a spelling checker, look for homonyms, and vary sentence structure. Students will make revisions to increase sentence complexity and use a thesaurus to enhance vocabulary and eliminate overused words.

Materials Needed

Structured Writing II CD-ROM

- Basic Book Report Web
- Basic Book Report Organizer

Inspiration 6.0 or 7.0

Word processing program

Posters

- Basic Book Report Web
- Biography Book Report Web
- Expanded Book Report Web
- Editing Steps (chapter 1)

Essential Elements

The Structured Writing II process teaches students to write a three-paragraph book report using:

1. An **introductory paragraph** containing the required information
2. One **body paragraph** describing the story plot
3. A **concluding paragraph** expressing the writer's opinion

Color Codes

- White for the book report title
- Blue for paragraph types
- Yellow for introductory and concluding sentences
- Green for supporting sentences
- Pink for details and elaboration

The Structured Writing II Process

Planning step: Outline the book report.

Writing step: Expand ideas into sentences. Organize sentences into paragraphs.

Editing step: Edit and revise one paragraph at a time.

Formatting step: Create a draft in book report format.

Publishing step: Print the final copy.

The Editing Process

1. Open the organizer file.
2. Use text-to-speech to read and listen to each sentence, one at a time, to check content. Edit and revise.
3. Check capitalization.
4. Check punctuation.
5. Check for homonyms and misused words.
6. Run a spelling checker.
7. Read and listen to changes using text-to-speech.
8. Save changes.
9. Print in color or print and highlight by hand.
10. Give to a proofreader for review.
11. Make any necessary changes suggested by the proofreader.
12. Submit to the teacher for feedback and approval.

The Basic Book Report Lesson Process

The Planning Step

Students begin the planning step by opening the Inspiration Basic Book Report Web template available on the CD-ROM accompanying this book. It is also reproduced in poster form on the following page. This template assists students in planning a book report by indicating the required information and the place to record it. The color code and text identify the essential parts of the book report: an information paragraph, a story plot paragraph, and an opinion paragraph. They also identify the essential elements of each paragraph: topic sentence, supporting sentences, and concluding sentence. The Notes feature in Inspiration contains definitions of literary terms, the required information, and questions to prompt the writer. These notes **must be hidden** before the outline is printed (see chapter 3 for instructions on hiding notes).

Teachers should model the lesson by assigning a book report on a completed class novel. This instruction models the book report using *The War With Grandpa*. Direct students to open the Basic Book Report Web template and identify the three paragraphs and their functions. For each paragraph, read the text boxes and identify the necessary information. Look at each paragraph with the class, one at a time, and identify the purpose of each. Discuss new literary terms and their meanings, and identify specific information from the novel. Point out to students that the entire report is made up of three separate paragraphs. The following list provides directions for completing the planning step.

1. Students open the Basic Book Report Web. The white box in the web indicates the place for the book report title. The blue ovals identify the paragraph types within the book report. The yellow boxes are for topic and concluding sentence ideas. The green boxes signify the place for supporting sentence ideas. The pink boxes are for the details about the supporting ideas.

2. Students type only key words and short phrases in the web to represent their ideas. **Reinforce the distinction between organizing ideas by outlining and actually writing sentences.** It is not the time to write complete sentences. It is imperative that students organize their ideas for the entire book report before beginning the writing step. While modeling, review literary terms such as genre and setting to familiarize students with new vocabulary and ensure their understanding. Figure 43 shows the Basic Book Report Web with the ideas filled in.

3. When all boxes are completed, students convert the web into a color-coded outline by selecting the Outline option in Inspiration. If changes need to be made in the order of the information, it is easier to rearrange in the outline format. Students run the spelling checker and save the outline as "book report title.outline" in the appropriate folder or directory. Figure 44 shows the Basic Book Report Outline template.

4. Some students may be overwhelmed or distracted by the entire essay while working on individual paragraphs. To simplify the visuals, simply choose Hide Subtopics in the Inspiration outline format and let students view only one paragraph at a time while they write.

5. When students are ready to print their outlines, they must first go to View in the main menu, then to Notes, and check Hide All to hide the notes on the outline. Then, students go to File in the main menu, scroll to Page Setup, and unchck Hidden Notes (see chapter 3 for more information). These steps will keep the notes from appearing on

Basic Book Report Web

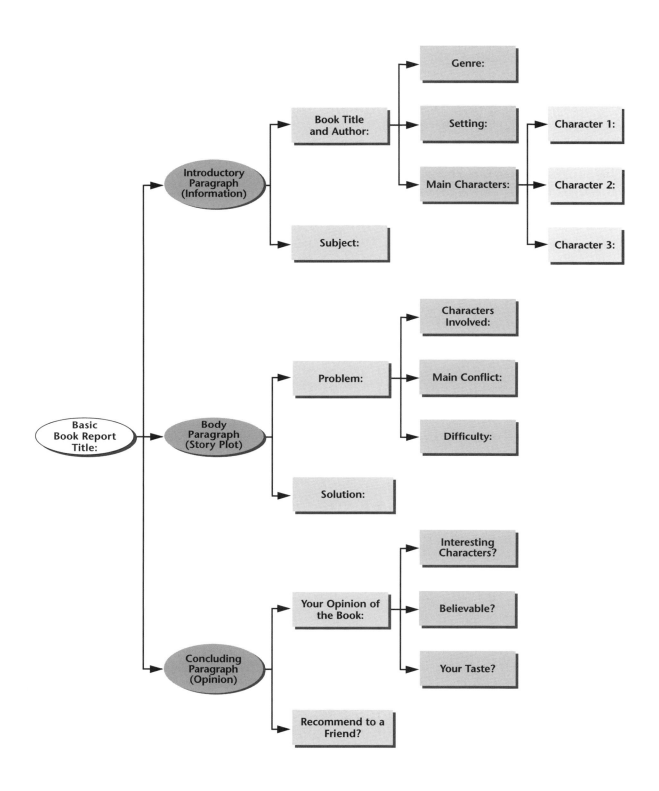

Basic Book Report Web Example

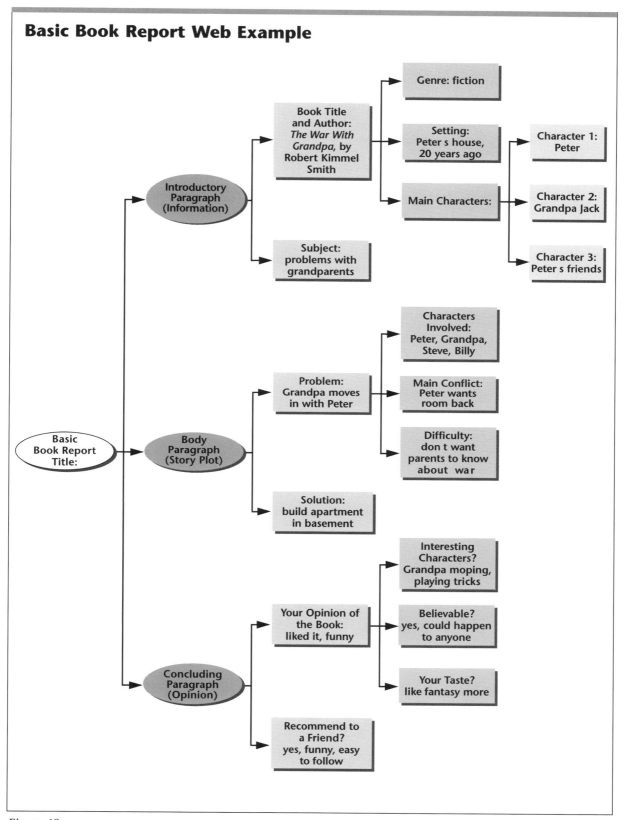

Figure 43.

Basic Book Report Outline

Title:

Introductory Paragraph (Information)

    A. Book Title and Author:

        1. Genre: *What type of story is this? Fiction (not true) or nonfiction (true)*

        2. Setting: *Where does the story take place? When?*

        3. Main Characters: *Who are they? Does anyone change (from bad to good, etc.) in the story? Who does the "right" thing?*

            a. Character 1: *Who/what is the most important character?*

            b. Character 2: *What is this character's role in the story?*

            c. Character 3: *What is this character's role in the story?*

    B. Subject: *What is the story about? General statement.*

Body Paragraph (Story Plot)

    A. Problem: *Element/problem around which action is centered.*

        1. Characters Involved: *Who is involved in the problem? How/why?*

        2. Main Conflict: *What problem needs to be solved?*

        3. Difficulty: *What/who gets in the way of solving the problem?*

    B. Solution: *How is the conflict solved?*

Concluding Paragraph (Opinion)

    A. Your Opinion of the Book: *Did you like/dislike the story. Why/why not?*

        1. Interesting Characters? *Did you like/dislike the characters?*

        2. Believable? *Any surprises?*

        3. Your Taste? *Like this genre?*

    B. Recommend to a Friend? *Clincher sentence. Who else might like this story?*

Figure 44. The Basic Book Report Outline template has notes to prompt the student.

the printed document. Figure 45 shows the Basic Book Report Outline without the notes showing.

6. Students print the color-coded outline or print it and highlight it by hand.

7. Students submit the outline to the teacher for review.

The teacher checks for content, order, and completeness to give feedback to the students before they begin the writing step. Reassured that they are on the right track, students use the outline to guide their efforts when writing.

The Writing Step

Students open the Structured Writing II Basic Book Report Organizer in their word processing program to begin the writing step (Figure 46). They expand their ideas from the outline into complete sentences in the organizer.

1. Students begin with the information paragraph. Here they compose a topic sentence that indicates their point of view concerning the value of the book. The teacher models a way to compose a sentence that combines the book title and author's name. The genre of the book is identified and recorded in a complete sentence. The subject can be modeled and expressed as a compound sentence that identifies both the theme of the story and the writer's attitude and feelings about the work. With both of these components expressed, the tone of the book report can be set and reiterated in the concluding (opinion) paragraph.

2. Students expand and elaborate their sentences one at a time in the writing step as they have done on many occasions using the Structured Writing process. When each required sentence is complete, teachers direct students to add transitions to the supporting sentences that will guide the reader through the main points in each paragraph.

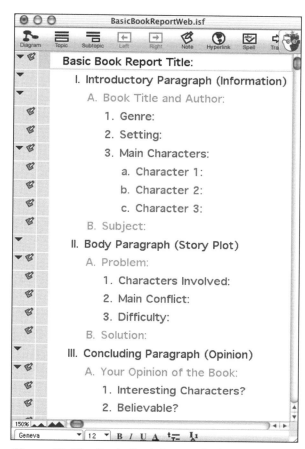

Figure 45. The Basic Book Report Outline without the notes showing.

3. Teachers instruct students to add adjective and adverb modifiers and prepositional phrases to elaborate and clarify their communication. They direct students to combine simple sentences into compound sentences and to vary the types and kinds of sentences used depending on the students' level and experience.

4. Teachers demonstrate ways to consult a thesaurus to eliminate overused words and to improve the complexity of written vocabulary.

5. Students save their files as "book report title.organizer."

Each paragraph is further refined in the editing step, one paragraph at a time.

The Editing Step

Students are required to use the Structured Writing editing process to make sure their sentences and paragraphs reflect the intended meaning and to correct spelling and mechanical errors. This step is more complex when editing a multi-paragraph document. Encourage students to consult the Editing Steps poster (chapter 1) to remind them of the procedures.

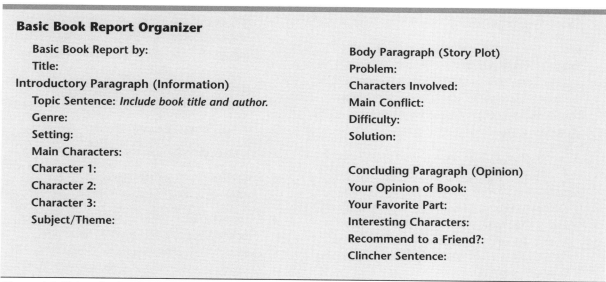

Figure 46. Using the Basic Book Report Organizer helps students apply literary terms to a book.

Example Edited Basic Book Report Organizer

Basic Book Report by: Student Name

Title: *The War With Grandpa* Book Report

Introductory Paragraph (Information)

Topic Sentence: The practical jokes Peter Stokes and his grandfather play on each other add humor and compassion to *The War With Grandpa,* written by Robert Kimmel Smith.

Genre: The genre of the book is fiction.

Setting: The setting is Peter's house somewhere in America about twenty years ago.

Main Characters: The main characters are Peter Stokes, his Grandpa Jack, and his friends, Steve and Billy.

Character 1: Peter is ten years old and has lived in his bedroom for his whole life.

Character 2: Grandpa Jack has a bad leg and is sad and lonely since Grandma died.

Character 3: Steve and Billy are Peter's friends who know about the secret "war" and give Peter questionable advice.

Subject/Theme: The story is about some of the problems that arise when grandparents move in with families, and shows the reader that most problems have solutions.

Body Paragraph (Story Plot)

Problem: The problem in the story revolves around who gets Peter's room.

Characters Involved: Peter and Grandpa play tricks on each other in their war.

Main Conflict: The main conflict is that Grandpa is in Peter's room, and Peter wants it back!

Difficulty: Peter has to keep the war secret from his parents or he will get in big trouble.

Solution: The problem is solved when Peter's father lets Grandpa turn his basement office into an apartment, and Grandpa moves in there.

Concluding Paragraph (Opinion)

Opinion of Book: I really liked the book because it was funny.

Your Favorite Part: My favorite part was when Grandpa hid all Peter's clothes and almost made him late for school.

Interesting Characters: Steve and Billy were very interesting characters because they were like my real friends.

Recommend to a Friend?: I would recommend this book to my friends because it is funny and easy to read.

Clincher Sentence: If you like funny stories filled with action, then you'll want to read *The War With Grandpa!*

Figure 47. This student is writing about The War With Grandpa.

1. Students open the saved organizer file, "book report title.organizer."

2. Students use text-to-speech to read and listen to each sentence, one at a time, within each paragraph. Here students add, delete, and change words until sentences sound right and the required information is communicated.

   ◆ Students make sure the required paragraphs for the basic book report are in the proper order and provide the necessary information within the Basic Book Report Organizer. They check each paragraph for proper structure (topic sentence, supporting sentences, transition words, details, and concluding sentence), and revise sentences to refine the paragraphs.

   ◆ Teachers instruct students to vary the structure of their sentences and use various kinds of sentences (declarative, imperative, exclamatory, interrogative), taking into account the skill level of the students. Teachers encourage students to combine simple sentences effectively into compound and complex sentences.

3. Students check capitalization.

4. Students check punctuation.

5. Students check word usage, including homonyms and misused words.

6. Students check spelling. Using the spelling checker after the other edits have been made gives students a better chance to properly correct misspelled words.

7. Students read and listen to changes using text-to-speech.

8. Students save each of the edited paragraphs within the book report organizer as "book report title.organizer" in the appropriate folder or directory. Each subsequent paragraph will be added to the basic book report when the paragraph is saved as "book report title.organizer," replacing the previous version.

9. Students print the edited organizer in color or print it and highlight it by hand.

10. Students give the document to a proofreader for review.

11. Students make any necessary changes suggested by the proofreader.

12. Students submit the document to the teacher for feedback and approval.

The teacher assesses the sentences for structure, variation, use of transition words, and proper syntax to give feedback to the students. Once the edited organizer (Figure 47) is approved, students move on to the formatting step.

The Formatting Step

In this step, students prepare the document for publishing. They remove the structure cues from the organizer, put the sentences into paragraph form, and combine the separate paragraphs into a multi-paragraph book report. The color code remains to reinforce paragraph structure within the report.

1. Students put the required heading on the document, such as their name and the date.

2. Students highlight the structure cues and delete them. As each structure cue is deleted, students arrange the sentences one after the other, paying attention to beginning capitalization, ending punctuation, and spacing between lines and sentences.

3. Students center the basic book report title, checking it for proper capitalization. They indent the topic sentence in the information paragraph and then the following paragraphs.

4. When all three paragraphs are put into the correct format with the color code intact, students read and listen again to the document as a whole.

5. Students save the document as "book report title.draft" in the proper folder or directory.

6. Students print the document in color or print it and highlight it by hand.

7. Students submit the draft to a proofreader for review.

The book report in Figure 48 was a "first," written by a fourth grade student with dyslexia after independently reading a "real chapter book." He had one year of experience with the Structured Writing process when he wrote this basic book report. He could verbally embellish every section of the template, yet his written expression was initially less elaborate. Once he understood the structure of the various book reports, he realized where to put the plethora of information he had accumulated. His subsequent book reports reflected the logical sequence of his thoughts, and his written explanations continue to "show what he really knows."

The Publishing Step

When students' drafts are approved, the writing process is complete except for removing the color code and printing a final copy.

1. Students consider the proofreader's suggestions and make the necessary corrections. When any changes are made, students reread and run another spelling check before resubmitting to a proofreader.

2. Students then change the text color to black.

Student Name
Date

The War With Grandpa **Book Report**

The practical jokes Peter Stokes and his grandfather play on each other add humor and compassion to *The War With Grandpa,* written by Robert Kimmel Smith. The genre of the book is fiction. The setting is Peter's house somewhere in America about twenty years ago. The main characters are Peter Stokes, his Grandpa Jack, and his friends, Steve and Billy. Peter is ten years old and has lived in his bedroom for his whole life. Grandpa Jack has a bad leg and is sad and lonely since Grandma died. Steve and Billy are Peter's friends who know about the secret "war" and give Peter questionable advice. The story is about some of the problems that arise when grandparents move in with families, and shows the reader that most problems have solutions.

The problem in the story revolves around who gets Peter's room. Peter and Grandpa play tricks on each other in their war. The main conflict is that Grandpa is in Peter's room, and Peter wants it back! Peter has to keep the war secret from his parents or he will get in big trouble. The problem is solved when Peter's father lets Grandpa turn his basement office into an apartment, and Grandpa moves in there.

I really liked the book because it was funny. My favorite part was when Grandpa hid all Peter's clothes and almost made him late for school. Steve and Billy were very interesting characters because they were like my real friends. I would recommend this book to my friends because it is funny and easy to read. If you like funny stories filled with action, then you'll want to read *The War With Grandpa!*

Figure 48. A Basic Book Report draft.

3. Students save the document in the appropriate folder or directory as "book report title.final copy."

4. Students print a final copy in black.

5. The authors submit to the teacher a complete packet containing the outline, organizer, draft, and final copy.

Summary

In summary, the Basic Book Report Lesson combines three specific paragraphs into one book report that includes:

1. An **introductory paragraph** (required information)

2. A **body paragraph** (story plot)

3. A **concluding paragraph** (opinion)

Each individual paragraph is written one at a time, conforming to the Structured Writing process. Teachers point out that individual paragraphs have a specific purpose within a book report. Each paragraph is written and edited, one at a time, within the specific book report organizer.

Writing a book report one paragraph at a time breaks the process into manageable parts. It is essential to model the book report using a novel the whole class has read. Many times students fail to remember that each paragraph has a purpose and put all of their information into one large paragraph. Active modeling with plenty of discussion seems to alleviate this confusion.

Evaluation Rubric

The Book Report Rubric focuses on student aptitude in following and filling out the book report template. Students must be accurate and provide an opinion. Content is specifically assessed for a direct and supportable thesis/focus sentence, supporting paragraphs that provide relevant information and appropriate elaboration, and ideas that are expressed in the writer's own words. Writing mechanics, sentence structure, and the use of technology to independently edit the written reports are also evaluated.

Book Report Rubric

STRUCTURE	EMERGING	DEVELOPING	PROFICIENT
Introduction/ Information	Introductory paragraph contains: ◆ Required information	Introductory paragraph contains: ◆ Required information ◆ Opinion-based thesis/focus sentence	Introductory paragraph contains: ◆ Required information ◆ Opinion-based thesis/focus sentence ◆ All elements of assigned format with improved presentation
Body	Supporting paragraphs: ◆ Provide required information ◆ Clearly relate to the thesis/focus sentence	Supporting paragraphs: ◆ Provide required information ◆ Clearly relate to the thesis/focus sentence	Supporting paragraphs: ◆ Provide required information ◆ Clearly relate to the thesis/focus sentence ◆ Are linked with effective transitions
Conclusion	Concluding paragraph: ◆ Contains required information	Concluding paragraph: ◆ Contains required information ◆ Refers to thesis/focus sentences	Concluding paragraph: ◆ Contains required information ◆ Refers to thesis/focus sentences ◆ Uses effective closing techniques

MECHANICS	EMERGING	DEVELOPING	PROFICIENT
Capitalization	Correct capitalization of: ◆ Sentences	Correct capitalization of: ◆ Sentences ◆ Proper nouns	Correct capitalization of: ◆ Sentences ◆ Proper nouns ◆ Titles ◆ Quotations
Punctuation	Correct use of: ◆ Sentence-ending punctuation	Correct use of: ◆ Sentence-ending punctuation ◆ Quotation marks	Correct use of: ◆ Sentence-ending punctuation ◆ Quotation marks ◆ Commas ◆ Apostrophes
Spelling	Spelling is: ◆ Correct enough to read ◆ Inconsistently checked with spelling checker	Spelling is: ◆ Correct ◆ Effectively checked with spelling checker ◆ Checked with text-to-speech feature	Spelling is: ◆ Correct ◆ Effectively checked with spelling checker ◆ Checked with text-to-speech feature ◆ Correct for homonyms and proper nouns

Continued on next page

Book Report Rubric, continued

MECHANICS	EMERGING	DEVELOPING	PROFICIENT
Sentence Structure	Sentences: ◆ Are structurally correct	Sentences: ◆ Are structurally correct ◆ Begin in various ways ◆ Contain diverse modifiers ◆ Include appropriate transition words	Sentences: ◆ Are structurally correct ◆ Begin in various ways ◆ Contain diverse modifiers ◆ Include appropriate transition words ◆ Vary in length ◆ Include compoud and complex syntax

CONTENT	EMERGING	DEVELOPING	PROFICIENT
Thesis/Focus Sentence	Thesis/focus sentence is: ◆ Direct	Thesis/focus sentence is: ◆ Direct ◆ Opinion-based	Thesis/focus sentence is: ◆ Direct ◆ Opinion-based ◆ Supportable ◆ Personal
Supporting Paragraphs	Supporting paragraphs: ◆ Include required information	Supporting paragraphs: ◆ Include required information ◆ Expand on thesis/focus sentence	Supporting paragraphs: ◆ Include required information ◆ Expand on thesis/focus sentence ◆ Creatively link topics
Facts/ Elaboration	Facts are: ◆ Accurate	Facts are: ◆ Accurate ◆ Appropriate ◆ Substantiated	Facts are: ◆ Accurate ◆ Appropriate ◆ Substantiated ◆ Personal
Style	Ideas are: ◆ Presented in the writer's own words	Ideas are: ◆ Presented in the writer's own words ◆ Explicit and clear	Ideas are: ◆ Presented in the writer's own words ◆ Explicit and clear ◆ Expressed by specific nouns and strong verbs ◆ Clearly original

The Biography Book Report Lesson Process

Students continue to use the Structured Writing II process to compose the more complex book reports. Teachers emphasize content and complexity, allowing the built-in structure of the Structured Writing II webs to reinforce the essential information required in each paragraph for a specific essay or report.

The biography book report follows the same process as the basic book report. Because it is a review about a work of nonfiction, the elements of fiction are not addressed. The writer's objective is to report on a story about a real person's life in an enlightening and engaging way. One may admire someone, be fascinated by his or her achievements, or find his or her circumstances curious. The Biography Book Report Web template is available on the CD-ROM accompanying this book. It is also reproduced in poster form on the following page.

The Biography Book Report Lesson is modeled here using *Mr. Blue Jeans—A Story About Levi Strauss*. Direct students to the Biography Book Report Web template and identify the three paragraphs and their functions. For each paragraph, read the text boxes and identify the necessary information. Look at each paragraph with the class, one at a time, and identify the purpose of each. Discuss the language used and what it means to identify specific information from the novel. Point out to students that the entire report is made up of three separate paragraphs.

Following the Structured Writing process, students fill in the web. An example completed web is reproduced in poster form on the foldout page at the end of this chapter. Discuss and review the person's significance and accomplishments from the biography. Familiarize students with new vocabulary to ensure their understanding. Students convert the web into a color-coded outline (Figure 49).

Students then open the Basic Book Report Organizer in their word processing program to begin the writing step. They expand their ideas from the outline into complete sentences in the organizer. After editing the organizer in the editing step, they remove the structure cues from the organizer, put the sentences into paragraph form, and combine the separate paragraphs into a multi-paragraph book report form in the formatting step.

Figure 50 shows a biography book report written by an eighth-grade girl with dyslexia. She had approximately two years of experience using the Structured Writing process when she wrote this. She was researching American fashion design when she came upon a biography about Levi Strauss. She used her biography book report as the basis for her PowerPoint presentation, "Rags to Riches." Her ultimate point was: now, it takes "riches" to buy "rags"!

Biography Book Report Web

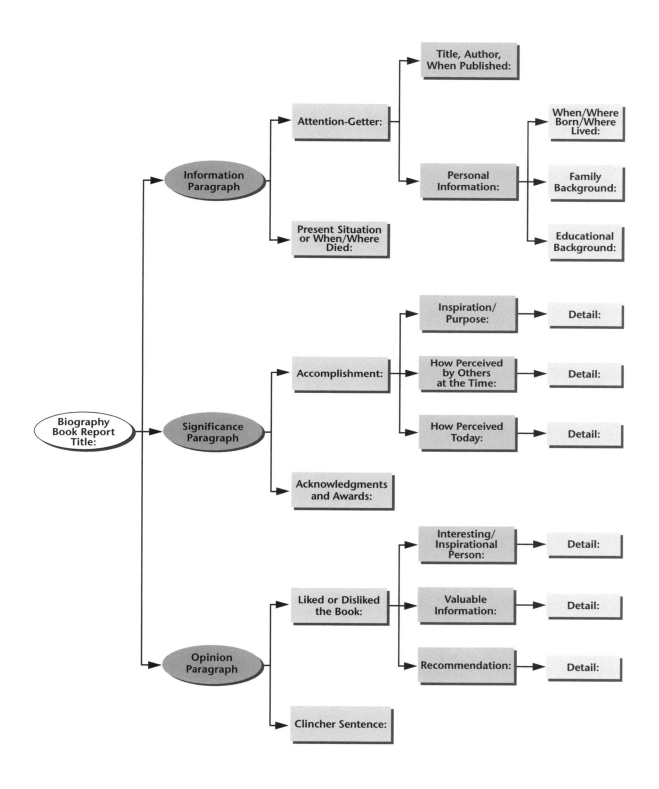

Example Biography Book Report Outline

I. **Title:** *Mr. Blue Jeans—A Story About Levi Strauss* Book Report

II. **Information Paragraph**

  A. **Attention-Getter:** Levi's an American phenomenon, rags-to-riches story

    1. **Title, Author, When Published:** *Mr. Blue Jeans—A Story About Levi Strauss,* by Maryann N. Weidt, 1990.

    2. **Personal Information:**

      a. **When/Where Born/Where Lived:** Lob Strauss, Buttenheim (Bavaria), 1829, Jewish

      b. **Family Background:** Father dry goods peddler, died when 16, took over his work. Gold in American streets. June 1847 left for U.S. American name Levi, lived in NY, didn't know English.

      c. **Educational Background:** Peddler in NYC, brothers had shop, then country, San Francisco for Gold Rush, take a risk. Around horn, sold bolts of fabric for gold nuggets. Business with brothers in law, cloth from brothers.

  B. **Present Situation or When/Where Died:** September 26, 1902

III. **Significance Paragraph**

  A. **Accomplishment:** Tough trousers—"Those pants of Levi's," Levi Strauss & Co.

    1. **Inspiration/Purpose:** miners' pants with riveted pockets to hold gold nuggets

      a. **Detail:** pants for railroad workers, cowboys, farmers' overalls

    2. **How Perceived by Others at the Time:** 1860, men everywhere wearing them, respected businessmen

      a. **Detail:** high regard dry goods, greeted employees by name

    3. **How Perceived Today:** creator of blue jeans 501s

      a. **Detail:** all makes sense once you know his story

  B. **Acknowledgments and Awards:** Levi's popular and classic garment named after the man

IV. **Opinion Paragraph**

  A. **Liked or Disliked the Book:** Really enjoyed interesting trivia

    1. **Interesting/Inspirational Person:** lucky, hard worker, honest, good businessman

      a. **Detail:** like reading about real people, learn history

    2. **Valuable Information:** de Nimes, rivets, Genoa trademarks

      a. **Detail:** fabric of denim, jeans from Genoa, rivets 1870; 501 lot number of fabric, orange thread to match copper rivets on back pockets seagull wings; 1886 leather patch on waistband 2 horses trying to tear apart pair of jeans; 1936—red and white tab Levi's right back pocket.

    3. **Recommendation:** Quick read, fashion conscious or interested in trivia from Gold Rush—all general interest

      a. **Detail:** Jean wearers everywhere would enjoy this history.

  B. **Clincher Sentence:** Levi's are an American symbol like hot dogs and apple pie!

Figure 49. A Biography Book Report Outline filled in with details about Mr. Blue Jeans.

Student Name

Date

Mr. Blue Jeans—A Story About Levi Strauss Book Report

Have you ever taken a close look at your blue jeans? What did you notice? Well, prepare to take a closer look. *Mr. Blue Jeans—A Story About Levi Strauss* is a rags to riches biography written by Maryann N. Weidt and published in 1990. Lob (Levi) Strauss was born into a Jewish family of peddlers. He was born in 1829 in Buttenheim, an old village in Bavaria. His father was a dry goods peddler who died when Lob was sixteen years old. Lob took over his father's job to support his mother and sisters. Being Jewish and fearing suppression, he paid close attention to the stories of gold in American streets. In June 1847, he and his family moved to the land of freedom and opportunity and settled in New York. In America, he thrived. On September 26, 1902, after a long, successful life and career, Levi Strauss died in his sleep at the age of seventy-three.

Levi Strauss' most notable accomplishment is that he founded the finest and largest manufacturer of denim jeans. Traveling to San Francisco in hopes of seeing the legendary streets of gold, Levi went into the dry goods business with his brother-in-law. To increase sales from mining towns, Levi again became a peddler. It is said that a prospector asked Levi to make a pair of sturdy pants from the canvas he peddled. The pants had pockets big enough to hold gold nuggets, and pretty soon everyone wanted "those pants of Levi's." The rest is history. Levi Strauss was perceived as a respected businessman during his life. In 1860, traders spread the word about Levi's pants, and railroad workers, cowboys, and farmers were wearing them. Made in the French town of Nimes (de Nimes), the cloth was called denim in America. Pants made of this denim were popular with Genoese sailors and called "jeans" after the Italian city of Genoa. The company is still best known today for its 501 jeans. It remains a family owned company and makes a full line of clothing for men, women, and children. Levi Strauss is acknowledged for the name he gave to a pair of pants and his charitable acts. He was a multimillionaire who generously shared his wealth with others.

I thoroughly enjoyed learning about the history of blue jeans, Levi Strauss, and denim trivia. Levi Strauss personifies the hardworking, smart, and lucky businessman and immigrant who lived the American Dream. I enjoy reading about other people's lives. The Levi trademark information was especially interesting to me. I'll always check for the orange thread, leather patch, and red and white Levi's patch. This is a quick read for kids attracted to Gold Rush times and for general interest. Jean wearers everywhere might enjoy this history. Levi's are truly an American symbol like hot dogs, apple pie, and baseball!

Figure 50. A Biography Book Report draft.

The Expanded Book Report Lesson Process

The expanded book report increases the intricacy of the basic book report. It includes a comprehensive discussion of the elements of fiction: characterization, story plot, setting, and theme. The writer forms an opinion about the novel and then supports it with examples and details from the reading.

Students begin the planning step by opening the Expanded Book Report Web template. The template is available on the CD-ROM accompanying this book. It is also reproduced in poster form on the foldout page at the end of this chapter.

I suggest modeling the lesson using a book report on a completed class novel (in the example provided, *Guns for General Washington*). Direct students to the Expanded Book Report Web template and identify the various paragraphs and their functions. For each paragraph, read the text boxes and identify the necessary information. Scrutinize each paragraph with the class, and identify the purpose of each. Discuss new literary terms and their meanings, such as genre, protagonist, and theme, and identify specific information from the novel. Point out to students that the entire report is made up of five separate paragraphs.

Students fill in the web with the required information and convert it into an outline to guide their writing in the writing step (Figure 51).

Students then open the Expanded Book Report Organizer in their word processing program to begin the writing step. They expand their ideas from the outline into complete sentences in the organizer. After editing the organizer in the editing step, they remove the structure cues from the organizer, put the sentences into paragraph form, and combine the separate paragraphs into a multi-paragraph book report form in the formatting step.

Figure 52 shows a book report that is a compilation based on the writings of an eighth-grade class of students with dyslexia. They had approximately two years of experience with the Structured Writing process, and this was the culminating book report on a work of historical fiction. The students incorporated new literary terminology and expressed their thoughtful interpretations and understanding of a novel read together as a class.

Example Expanded Book Report Outline

I. **Title:** *Guns for General Washington* Book Report

II. **Information Paragraph**

  A. **Thesis/Focus Sentence:** *Offer thoughts to explain, defend, and discuss your perspective. Include the theme—the message about life and human nature that is "hidden" in the story.*

    story of the Ticonderoga Cannon Convoy revealing the vision, passion, and determination of young American Patriots

    1. **Title, Author, When Published:** *Guns for General Washington,* by Seymour Reit, 1990.

      a. **Genre:** *Fiction, nonfiction, historical fiction, fantasy, biography, etc.*
      historical fiction

      b. **Point of View From Which the Story Is Told:**

        ◆ *First person: One of the characters is telling the story.*

        ◆ *Third person: Somebody from outside the story is telling it.*

        ◆ *Omniscient point of view: Knows thoughts and feelings of all characters.*

        ◆ *Limited omniscient point of view: Shares thoughts and feelings of one character.*

        ◆ *Camera view: When storyteller tells from his or her point of view, unaware of other characters' feelings.*

        third person narration omniscient point of view

  B. **Setting:** *Describe the place and time frame in which the story takes place. Does it significantly affect characters or increase your knowledge of a certain time in history?*

    Boston, winter, British have control of the harbor; upstate New York during American Revolution

III. **Characterization Paragraph**

  A. **Main Characters:** *Many or few? Do they stay the same throughout the story or change? Are they believable?*

    two groups of characters: Americans and British in Revolutionary War

    1. **Protagonist:** *The main character in the story, often a good or heroic type. ___ does the right thing when . . .*

    Colonel Henry Knox, Patriot

      a. **Physical Characteristics:** *Describe features that help to identify this character.*
      25, 6 ft. tall, quick and agile

      b. **Personality Traits:** *Describe distinguishing behaviors of this character.*
      daring, courageous, booming laugh, shares credit with convoy

      c. **Human Dynamics:** *Describe the role and relationship to other characters. This character changes from ____ to ____ by the end of the story.*
      inspirational, optimistic, convinces Washington, leads convoy, others doubtful

    2. **Antagonist:** *The person or force that works against the hero of the story.*

    Will Knox, younger brother

      a. **Physical Characteristics:** *Describe feature that help to identify this character.*
      19 years old

      b. **Personality Traits:** *Describe distinguishing behaviors of this character.*
      anxious to "do something" about the British, brave, risk taker, trustworthy

      c. **Human Dynamics:** *Describe the role and relationship to other characters.*
      grows up on journey, leads others

    3. **Foil Character:** *The person who serves as a contrast or challenges the main character.*

    General Washington

      a. **Physical Characteristics:** *Describe features that help to identify this character.*
      tall, elegant, white wig, striking figure on horse

      b. **Personality Traits:** *Describe distinguishing behaviors of this character.*
      professional soldier and leader, takes chance with Knox

      c. **Human Dynamics:** *Describe the role and relationship to other characters.*
      delegates responsibility to Knox brothers, supports efforts against odds

    4. **Other Character:**

    General William Howe, British "Bow Wow Howe"

      a. **Physical Characteristics:** *Describe features that help to identify this character.*
      tall, dark, dignified

      b. **Personality Traits:** *Describe distinguishing behaviors of this character.*
      professional, exacting, demanding

      c. **Human Dynamics:** *Describe the role and relationship to other characters.*
      respected leader of British, strategist, against Washington—lives up to deal

Continued on next page

Figure 51. In this Expanded Book Report Outline, extended notes appear in italics.

Example Expanded Book Report Outline, continued

B. **Theme:** *Discuss the message about life or human nature that is "hidden" in the story that the writer tells. Connect to focus statement.*

Ingenuity and determination of human spirit made America.

IV. **Story Plot**

A. **Main Conflict:** *A problem or struggle between two opposing forces in a story.*

Americans and British in stalemate in Boston— nothing can get in or out—need British out

1. **Basic Conflict:**

   ◆ *Person against Person: A problem between characters.*

   ◆ *Person against Self: A problem within a character's own mind.*

   ◆ *Person against Society: A problem between a character and society, school, the law, or some tradition.*

   ◆ *Person against Nature: A problem between a character and some element of nature: blizzard, hurricane, etc.*

   ◆ *Person against Fate or God: A problem or struggle that appears to be well beyond the character's control.*

   Person vs. nature: Get artillery from Ticonderoga to Boston in middle of winter.

   a. **Characters Involved and Human Dynamics:** *Static, unchanging? Dynamic, changing?*

   Henry & Will Knox, the cannon convoy work together

2. **Rising Action:** *The central part of the story during which various problems arise.*

   travel over perilous terrain, get to Boston secretly and in time

   a. **Issues to Resolve:**
   crossing Lakes Champlain & George, melting ice, craggy cliffs, mud, blizzards

3. **Climax:** *The high point in the action of a story.*

   surprise setup of Patriot cannons on Dorchester Heights

   a. **Characters Involved:** *Who does what?*
   work in dark at night, use straw to silence carwheels, build fascines, set up forts

   b. **Main Turning Point:**
   British fooled and beat when they notice "new" defensive forts next morning

4. **Falling Action:** *The action and dialogue following the climax that lead the reader into the story's end.*

   cannons "speak," British posture

   a. **Characters Involved:**
   Generals Washington & Howe

B. **Resolution:** *The part in the story in which the problems are solved and the action comes to a satisfying end.*

Howe doesn't level Boston and Washington doesn't sink British fleet.

V. **Opinion Paragraph**

A. **Your Favorite Part of the Story:**

1. **Reasons:** *Characterization? Could you identify with a character? Author's style).*

   described different things for protection like fascines, made me feel I was there

   a. **Detail:**
   tightly woven branches to hide cannons, protect from musket fire, barrels with rocks inside to roll downhill

2. **Believable?** *Use of descriptions; interesting vocabulary.*

   very understandable with the descriptions

   a. **Detail:**
   the protective devices were ingenious and workable

3. **Surprising Elements?:** *How author created suspense, tension, surprise.*

   tension with silence and number of people working so close to British

   a. **Detail:**
   wind blowing the other direction

B. **Overall Opinion:** *State your opinion of the whole story.*

marvelous adventure story that happens to be true

VI. **Concluding Paragraph**

A. **Recommendation:** *Who might enjoy reading this story?*

history buffs

1. **Appropriate Age:** *Specific reasons.*
   kids studying U.S. history to adults

   a. **Detail:**
   little known incident not in textbooks

2. **Reading Level:** *Specific examples and reasons.*
   6th—not too long, some old-fashioned words difficult

   a. **Detail:**
   use the map in the cover to help understand

3. **Taste:** *Your taste? Explain why the genre appeals to you or not.*
   prefer fantasy fiction, but loved this story and want to read more about American Revolution

   a. **Detail:**

B. **Clincher Sentence:** *Total effect on the reader.*
   What a way to learn about history!

Figure 51 (continued from previous page). The Expanded Book Report Outline.

Student Name

Date

Guns for General Washington **Book Report**

The true story of the Ticonderoga Cannon Convoy reveals the vision, passion, and determination of young American Patriots against all odds during the American Revolution. *Guns for General Washington,* written by Seymour Reit, was published in 1990. The genre is historical fiction. It is a third-person narration from the omniscient point of view. The setting is Boston during the winter of 1775 when the British Navy had control of the harbor. In an effort to remove the blockade, the convoy travels to Fort Ticonderoga in New York to bring needed artillery back to defend Boston.

Two American Patriots, General George Washington, and a British Naval Officer are the main characters in this story. Colonel Henry Knox, a trusted officer on General Washington's staff, is the protagonist in the story. He is a young man of twenty-five, six feet tall, who is quick and agile. He is a daring and courageous soldier with a booming laugh who shared credit for success with his men. Henry's creative plan and optimism convinced General Washington to give him a chance to try out a plan that others thought was daft. Second, Will Knox, Henry's younger brother, is another important character in the story. He is nineteen years old and a rebel at heart. He is brave, trustworthy, and eager to do something to help the cause against the British. Will grows up on the convoy and learns to be a leader of men like his brother. Next, General George Washington, the leader of the Continental Army, is another character crucial to the story. He is a tall, elegant man who wears a white wig and is a striking figure on a horse. Washington is a professional soldier and natural leader who takes a risk with Colonel Knox. General Washington entrusts responsibility to the Knox brothers and supports their efforts to find and transport the artillery in what others believe is an impossible task. In addition, General William Howe, "Bow Wow Howe," is the officer in charge of the British fleet that has blockaded Boston. He is a tall, dark, and dignified officer. He is exacting and demanding of his officers and soldiers. A respected leader of the British fleet, General Howe is an accomplished strategist who battles against General Washington and the Patriots. The theme of the story reveals and honors the courage, bravery, ingenuity, and determination of the human spirit that paved the way for the future of America.

The story plot revolves around the stalemate between the British Navy that controls the seaside and the American Patriots who are blockaded in Boston Harbor, but control the landside. The basic conflict is one of person against nature as Colonel Henry Knox and his brother, Will, take on the task of secretly moving cannons from Fort Ticonderoga to Boston during the dead of winter. Henry and Will Knox choose only rugged volunteers who work together as a successful convoy. The rising action occurs while the convoy secretly travels over the perilous terrain, trying to get to Boston in time to win the battle for the Americans. Moving heavy artillery across Lake George, dealing with a blizzard, melting ice at river crossings, knee-deep mud, and craggy cliffs were a few of the treacherous complications the convoy faced. The surprise setup of the Patriot cannons on Dorchester Heights was the climax of the story. The entire cannon convoy worked under cover of darkness, using straw to silence cart wheels, build fascines, create a parapet, and set up the defensive forts. Fooling the British was the main turning point in the story as threatening American forts "materialized" one morning, and the cannons "spoke." In the falling action, both the Americans and the British did some posturing to save face during the confrontation.

Continued on next page

Figure 52. An Expanded Book Report draft.

Generals Washington and Howe proved to be intelligent leaders who valued their men. The resolution occurred when General Howe and General Washington made a bargain: Howe did not destroy Boston, and in return Washington allowed the British to leave Boston Harbor unharmed.

My favorite part of the story was when the Rebels took the cannons up to Dorchester Heights. The descriptions of the ways the Patriots made protective barriers because the ground was frozen and they couldn't dig trenches made me feel like I was there. They built fascines that were bundles of tightly woven branches used to hide cannons and protect soldiers from musket fire. They also filled wooden barrels with sand and rocks to support the fascines that they could also roll down the hill at the British if necessary. The whole story was very understandable because of the descriptions. The original protective devices were ingenious and worked. The author created tension when describing the large number of soldiers trying to work silently so close to the British because if they discovered the scheme, they could have destroyed everything at once. It was easy to picture the straw on the ground, men whispering and using "blue" nightlights, and wind blowing in the opposite direction to help keep noise down. *Guns for General Washington* is a marvelous adventure story about the great cannon trek of 1775 that played a vital role in the American Revolution.

I certainly recommend this work of historical fiction for adventure and history buffs. It is appropriate reading for kids studying U.S. history and adults, too. The novel deals with a little-known incident from the American Revolution that is not discussed in textbooks. It is written at about a sixth-grade reading level with some old-fashioned words that are difficult because they are not easily found in the dictionary. The map in the cover of the book is helpful for under-standing the geography of the setting. Though I usually prefer to read fantasy fiction, I really enjoyed this story and want to read more about the American Revolution. Reading *Guns for General Washington* is a great way to learn about history!

Figure 52 (continued from previous page). An Expanded Book Report draft.

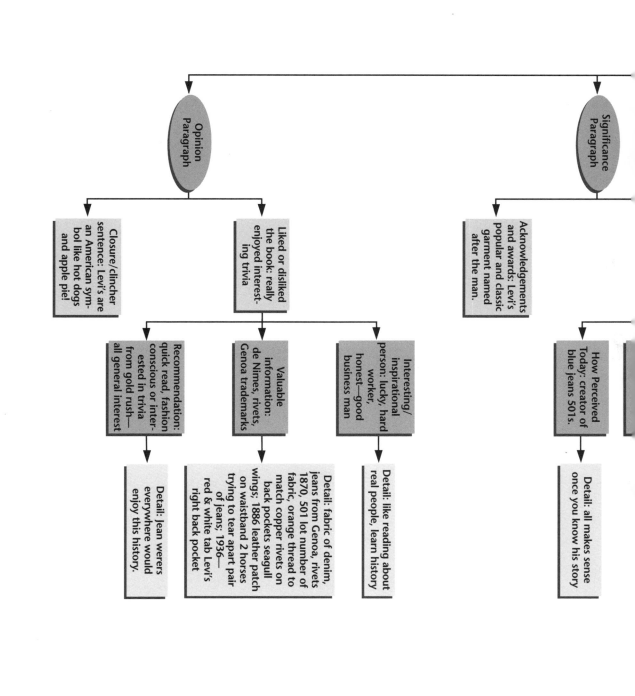

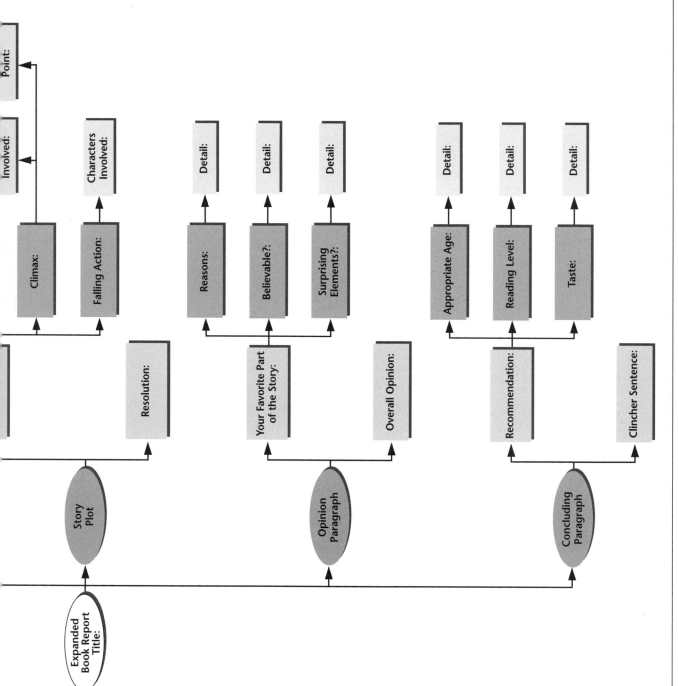

Expanded Book Report Web

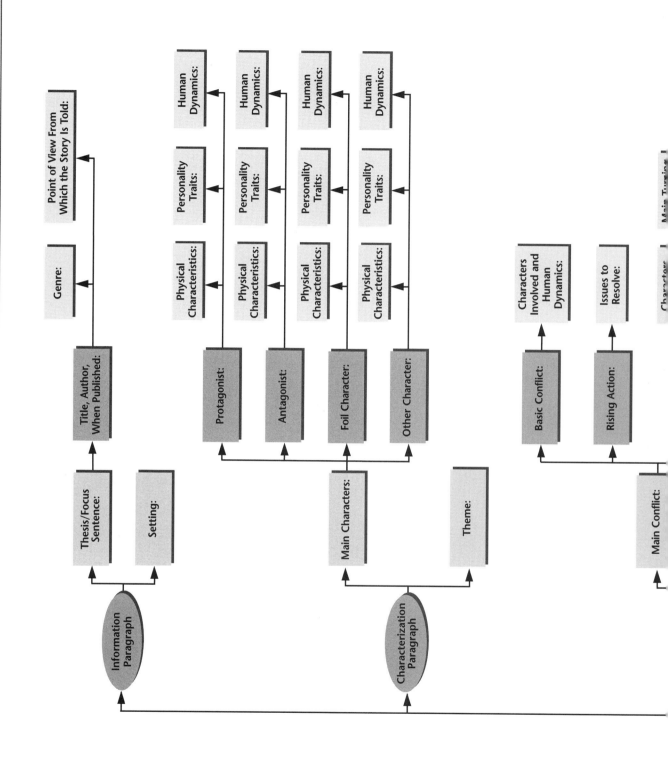

Biography Book Report Web Example

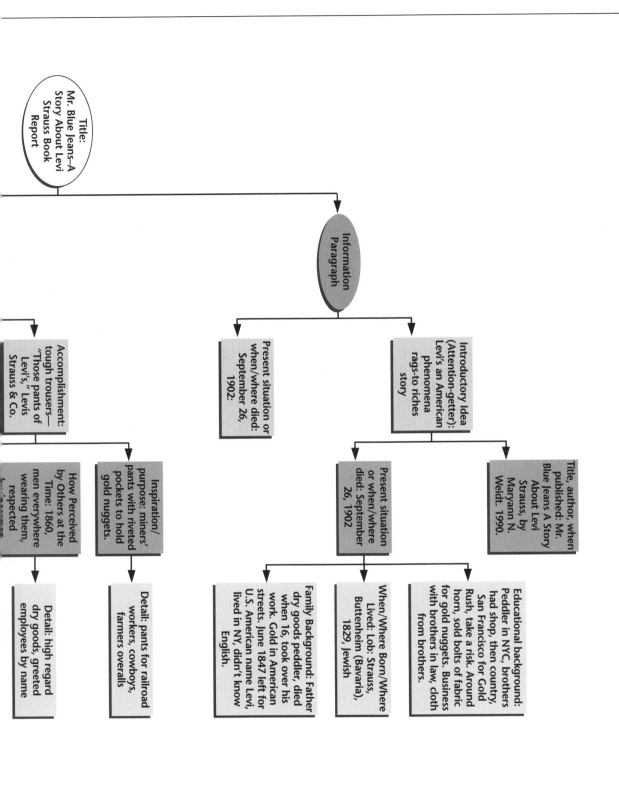

Title: Mr. Blue Jeans–A Story About Levi Strauss Book Report

Information Paragraph

Accomplishment: tough trousers—"Those pants of Levi's," Levis Strauss & Co.

Present situation or when/where died: September 26, 1902:

Introductory Idea (Attention-getter): Levi's an American phenomena rags-to riches story

Title, author, when published: Mr. Blue Jeans A Story About Levi Strauss, by Maryann N. Weidt. 1990.

How Perceived by Others at the Time: 1860, men everywhere wearing them, respected

Inspiration/ purpose: miners'/ pants with riveted pockets to hold gold nuggets.

Present situation or when/where died: September 26, 1902

Educational background: Peddler in NYC, brothers had shop, then country, San Francisco for Gold Rush, take a risk. Around horn, sold bolts of fabric for gold nuggets. Business with brothers in law, cloth from brothers.

When/Where Born/Where Lived: Lob: Strauss, Buttenheim (Bavaria), 1829, Jewish

Family Background: Father dry goods peddler, died when 16, took over his work. Gold in American streets. June 1847 left for U.S. American name Levi, lived in NY, didn't know English.

Detail: high regard dry goods, greeted employees by name

Detail: pants for railroad workers, cowboys, farmers overalls

Conclusion

Compared with writing a sentence or paragraph, writing an essay is a daunting task for many students. Writing an essay is made more manageable when the overall structure is clearly understood and it is written paragraph by paragraph. A specific, direct instruction method is the most likely path of success for students who struggle to write paragraphs and essays. Structured Writing is a step-by-step direct instruction method to deliver the writing process using technology tools for assistance. It begins by teaching the structure of basic paragraphs and progresses to more complex expository paragraphs. Students with experience using Structured Writing have learned to independently plan, compose, and edit various types of expository paragraphs.

When students have sufficient experience using the Structured Writing process to write expository paragraphs, they are ready to embark on the demanding task of writing essays and reports. The direct instruction method of Structured Writing clearly delineates the teacher's expectations for writing assignments and details the process that students must go through to successfully meet them. Structured Writing II expands this process to teach struggling students methods to effectively produce more complex essays and reports. Students use the process to plan, compose, edit, format, and publish properly ordered and detailed essays and reports.

During the instruction sequence, the writing process remains virtually the same: plan, write, edit, format, and publish. The sequence is the same for writing a single paragraph or a dense essay. Writing is similar to swimming. Once you learn to swim, you can in theory swim in water of any depth. The depth of the water may be intimidating, but if you continue to stroke, kick, and keep breathing, you will keep your head above water. Likewise, the writing process remains the same, regardless of whether you are assigned to write a paragraph or an essay. The more complex the writing assignment, the more intimidating it might be. One must trust the process to succeed.

The Structured Writing II process uses matched templates from Inspiration and organizers in a word processing program to provide a graphic view, give specific and direct instruction, and allow for the linear conversion necessary to organize an acceptable essay or book report. The color code identifies the fundamental parts of an essay and reinforces previously learned essential paragraph elements. The steps in the Structured Writing II process are:

- **Planning step:** An Inspiration web template is used to organize ideas and generate an outline to guide writing.

- **Writing step:** A word processing organizer is color-coded to match the Inspiration outline and allows students to expand and organize their ideas into a complete essay, one paragraph at a time. Students use transition sentences to link paragraphs within an essay.

◆ **Editing step:** Using the editing functions of a word processing program, the students check content and correct capitalization, punctuation, word usage, and spelling errors. They use specific nouns and strong verbs, appropriate modifiers, and a thesaurus to enhance vocabulary.

◆ **Formatting step:** The structure cues are removed from the document and the paragraphs are placed into essay draft form. Students reread their work to ensure that they have used appropriate transition words and sentences, then submit to a proofreader.

◆ **Publishing step:** After approval from a proofreader, the document is corrected, the color code is removed, and the essay is published as a final copy.

Structured Writing visually guides students to understand the structure and requirements of their writing assignments. The computer allows students to build the structural elements as an independent step and then easily expand and combine these elements into complex paragraphs, essays, and book reports.

During the past six years, I have used and developed the Structured Writing process with students with dyslexia ranging from the third- to eighth-grade levels. These students have inspired me to continue to expand the process to include essays and reports, and they have been my "guinea pigs." Their individual and collective suggestions have been incorporated into the vocabulary and sequence of the process. Their motivation and persistence have been tremendously encouraging. All of these students have significantly improved their expository writing skill, learning first how to structure and organize their writing, and then adding texture with their individual perspectives and writing styles.

As the course progresses, students learn to visually recognize the specific types and purposes of the various essays and reports. They differentiate between the essays and book reports to determine the type of essay needed to best explain a concept, answer a specific question, or write a particular book review. *Structured Writing* and *Structured Writing II* emphasize the process and reinforce good writing practices. Each new concept builds on what has been previously learned. All through the Structured Writing and Structured Writing II sequences, the expectations, content, quality, and quantity of writing increase. Combining effective writing instruction with word processing enhances students' writing.

Swimmers sometimes use inflatable paraphernalia to secure their buoyancy and fins to improve their competence in the water. Similarly, Structured Writing and Structured Writing II provide the needed scaffolding and equipment to improve students' writing competence and confidence. Use them as a springboard and dive into writing!

Appendix A

National Educational Technology Standards for Students (NETS•S)

The National Educational Technology Standards for Students are divided into six broad categories. Standards within each category are to be introduced, reinforced, and mastered by students. Teachers can use these standards as guidelines for planning technology-based activities in which students achieve success in learning, communication, and life skills.

1. Basic Operations and Concepts

Students:

A. demonstrate a sound understanding of the nature and operation of technology systems.

B. are proficient in the use of technology.

2. Social, Ethical, and Human Issues

Students:

A. understand the ethical, cultural, and societal issues related to technology.

B. practice responsible use of technology systems, information, and software.

C. develop positive attitudes toward technology uses that support lifelong learning, collaboration, personal pursuits, and productivity.

3. Technology Productivity Tools

Students:

A. use technology tools to enhance learning, increase productivity, and promote creativity.

B. use productivity tools to collaborate in constructing technology-enhanced models, preparing publications, and producing other creative works.

4. Technology Communications Tools

Students:

A. use telecommunications to collaborate, publish, and interact with peers, experts, and other audiences.

B. use a variety of media and formats to communicate information and ideas effectively to multiple audiences.

5. Technology Research Tools

Students:

A. use technology to locate, evaluate, and collect information from a variety of sources.

B. use technology tools to process data and report results.

C. evaluate and select new information resources and technological innovations based on the appropriateness to specific tasks.

6. Technology Problem-Solving and Decision-Making Tools

Students:

A. use technology resources for solving problems and making informed decisions.

B. employ technology in the development of strategies for solving problems in the real world.

Appendix B

National Educational Technology Standards for Teachers (NETS•T)

All classroom teachers should be prepared to meet the following standards and performance indicators.

I. Technology Operations and Concepts

Teachers demonstrate a sound understanding of technology operations and concepts. Teachers:

A. demonstrate introductory knowledge, skills, and understanding of concepts related to technology (as described in the ISTE National Educational Technology Standards for Students).

B. demonstrate continual growth in technology knowledge and skills to stay abreast of current and emerging technologies.

II. Planning and Designing Learning Environments and Experiences

Teachers plan and design effective learning environments and experiences supported by technology. Teachers:

A. design developmentally appropriate learning opportunities that apply technology-enhanced instructional strategies to support the diverse needs of learners.

B. apply current research on teaching and learning with technology when planning learning environments and experiences.

C. identify and locate technology resources and evaluate them for accuracy and suitability.

D. plan for the management of technology resources within the context of learning activities.

E. plan strategies to manage student learning in a technology-enhanced environment.

III. Teaching, Learning, and the Curriculum

Teachers implement curriculum plans that include methods and strategies for applying technology to maximize student learning. Teachers:

A. facilitate technology-enhanced experiences that address content standards and student technology standards.

B. use technology to support learner-centered strategies that address the diverse needs of students.

C. apply technology to develop students' higher order skills and creativity.

D. manage student learning activities in a technology-enhanced environment.

IV. Assessment and Evaluation

Teachers apply technology to facilitate a variety of effective assessment and evaluation strategies. Teachers:

A. apply technology in assessing student learning of subject matter using a variety of assessment techniques.

B. use technology resources to collect and analyze data, interpret results, and communicate findings to improve instructional practice and maximize student learning.

C. apply multiple methods of evaluation to determine students' appropriate use of technology resources for learning, communication, and productivity.

V. Productivity and Professional Practice

Teachers use technology to enhance their productivity and professional practice. Teachers:

A. use technology resources to engage in ongoing professional development and lifelong learning.

B. continually evaluate and reflect on professional practice to make informed decisions regarding the use of technology in support of student learning.

C. apply technology to increase productivity.

D. use technology to communicate and collaborate with peers, parents, and the larger community in order to nurture student learning.

VI. Social, Ethical, Legal, and Human Issues

Teachers understand the social, ethical, legal, and human issues surrounding the use of technology in PK–12 schools and apply that understanding in practice. Teachers:

A. model and teach legal and ethical practice related to technology use.

B. apply technology resources to enable and empower learners with diverse backgrounds, characteristics, and abilities.

C. identify and use technology resources that affirm diversity.

D. promote safe and healthy use of technology resources.

E. facilitate equitable access to technology resources for all students.